Advisory Group

The following were members of an Advisory Group established by the Gulbenkian Foundation which advised the authors:
Raymond Clarke, formerly Secretary of the Children's Committee
Paul Curno, Deputy Director, Calouste Gulbenkian Foundation, UK Branch
Baroness David, education spokesperson
Professor Nicholas Deakin, Head of Social Policy & Social Work Department, University of Birmingham
Baroness Ewart-Biggs, President, UNICEF-UK
Baroness Faithfull, Chair, All-Party Parliamentary Group for Children
Rachel Hodgkin, Children's Legal Centre
Dr Penelope Leach, child psychologist and author
Sir Peter Newsam, Director, University of London Institute of Education
John Rea Price, Director, National Children's Bureau
Ben Whitaker, Director, Calouste Gulbenkian Foundation, UK Branch

Acknowledgements

While the two of us bear entire responsibility for the contents of this report and such inadequacies and errors as it may contain, we tried throughout this project to ensure that our proposals gained maximum benefit from extensive discussion with a wide range of individuals and organisations. The effort spent on these consultations has undoubtedly been worthwhile several times over in terms of the resulting improvements, for which we are very grateful. None of those mentioned is of course in any way committed to what we made of their views.

We would like to thank:

● in particular the members of our Advisory Group for the time and thought they contributed;

● the following who kindly gave up their time to discuss our ideas with us: John Bash, Director of Investigations, Commission for Local Administration (England); Stephen Campbell, Association of County Councils; Sir Cecil Clothier QC, Chairman, Council on Tribunals; James Cornford; Navnit Dholakia, Jane Lane, Jackie Robinson & Liz Szondi, Commission for Racial Equality; Jenny Edwards; Målfrid Grude Flekkøy, Norwegian Children's Ombudsperson 1981-89; Jean Goose & Suzanne McCarthy, Home Office; Teresa Gorman MP; Kathy Ham; Brenda Hancock, Equal Opportunities Commission; Graeme Hitchen & Bernard Donoghue, British Youth Council; Prof Brenda Hoggett, Law Commission; Menachem Horovitz, Jerusalem Children's Ombudsperson 1986-90; Rupert Hughes & Anne Whittle, Department of Health; Gwen James, Voice for the Child in Care; Brian Jones, Association of Metropolitan Authorities; Elizabeth Lawson QC; Joan Lestor MP; Mike Lindsay, Leicestershire County Council Children's Rights Service; Mary Moss, National Association of Young People in Care; Michael Nicholls & Michael Hinchcliffe, Official Solicitor's Department; Louise Pankhurst, Child Accident Prevention Trust; Barry Pless, Canadian Institute of Child Health; Stephen Sedley QC; Baroness Serota; Sarah Spencer; Judge Stephen Tumim, HM Chief Inspector of Prisons; Sir William Utting, Chief Social Services Inspector; and Malcolm Wicks, Family Policy Studies Centre.

● the following organisations and individuals who sent us comments on our ideas: Barnardos; British Paediatric Association; Child Care/National Council of Voluntary Child Care Organisations; Child Care/NCVCCO Northern Ireland Group; ChildLine; Child Poverty Action Group; Children's Legal Centre;

Children's Society; Children's Society Wales Advocacy Unit; Convention of Scottish Local Authorities; Family Service Units; National Association for the Care and Resettlement of Offenders; National Association of Social Workers in Education; National Children's Centre; National Children's Home; National Consumer Council; National Foster Care Association; RADAR; Save the Children Fund; Voluntary Council for Handicapped Children; Who Cares?; and Who Cares? (Scotland); Prof John Griffith; Lord Henderson of Brompton KCB; Anthony Lester QC; and Prof Victor Moore.

● and the 30 organisations which operate complaints procedures or have similar or connected responsibilities and responded to our questionnaire on their use by children and young people (see appendix 3).

Last and far from least we are naturally extremely grateful to the Calouste Gulbenkian Foundation for funding the research and the report; and to its Deputy Director, Paul Curno (who oversees the Foundation's Social Welfare Programme from which our grant came), and its Director, Ben Whitaker, for their assistance and support.

Note

In this report the terms 'children' and 'children and young people' are used with the same meaning, to refer to everyone from birth and under 18, the legal age of majority in the UK.

Contents

Foreword

Children are, perhaps, the last major group in our society whose rights have yet to be fully recognised. As a result, their needs frequently take second place to the demands and requirements of other, more articulate minorities (or majorities), unless others press claims on their behalf.

With that in mind, in 1990 the Gulbenkian Foundation (UK Branch) declared a new priority, the Needs and Rights of Children and Young People, taking as a framework the UN Convention on the Rights of the Child, which is printed as an appendix to this report. In fact we went further, and one of our major initiatives during 1990 was to establish the basis for a Children's Rights Development Unit intended to promote the fullest possible implementation of the Convention in this country.

We were also concerned to explore with others how the needs and rights of children and young people might best be considered by national and local policy-making structures. We therefore commissioned the authors of this report, both of whom have extensive experience in the field of children's policy, to examine how progress could be made. To assist them, we also set up an advisory group of individuals who have a great deal of collective expertise in children's issues and public policy generally.

The ideas contained in the draft of this report were discussed widely with children's organisations and other interested individuals and agencies. The final version has thus benefited from the views of many people, and we are very grateful for their help.

While the Foundation itself is not in a position to advocate a particular proposal, it commends this report as a valuable contribution to public education and debate on this important topic.

Paul Curno
Deputy Director
Calouste Gulbenkian Foundation, UK Branch

Summary

This summarises the first three sections of the report: the introduction, the explanation of the need for a Children's Rights Commissioner, and the detailed proposal for one.

1. Introduction

This report proposes the creation of a 'Children's Rights Commissioner' - an independent statutory office to promote the rights and interests of children and young people.

In the past few years many people concerned about children and young people have recognised the need for some sort of organisation along these lines (see appendix 1). We were commissioned by the Calouste Gulbenkian Foundation to examine the idea in detail and produce a practical blueprint.

Creating such a Commissioner would be welcomed by many children's organisations, professional bodies and other interested groups.

In October 1990 the Scottish Child Care Law Review Group, established by the Secretary of State for Scotland, suggested that the similar idea of a 'Child Welfare Commission' should be examined. This is currently being considered by the Secretary of State.

Comparable ideas are being adopted internationally. Other countries such as Norway and New Zealand have already created official posts to promote children's rights. The Council of Europe is considering the best mechanisms for promoting children's rights in its member states. (See appendix 2.)

Creating a Children's Rights Commissioner would be in line with national and international trends towards greater recognition of children's rights.

2. The Need for a Children's Rights Commissioner

There is deep-seated and widespread concern that policy-making and practice often do not give enough recognition to children's rights and interests.

Why is it necessary to create an institution specifically for the benefit of children and young people? And what sort of institution should it be?

The need for action

● The United Nations Convention on the Rights of the Child will provide the Government with new obligations towards children and young people. The UK must ensure that the Convention is implemented on a long-term basis and that children's rights receive political priority.

● Our democracy is based on the premise that groups of people will stand up for their own interests and rights, but children are not in a position to do this. They do not vote or play a part in the political process which determines both nationally and locally the policies that affect their lives. As a result the impact of policies on children receives insufficient care and attention, children are a low political priority and issues are not looked at from a child's perspective.

● Government and local authority responsibilities for children's services are widely dispersed across different departments. The resulting lack of co-ordination has often been strongly criticised. There is no one with the authority to look across the board at how policy generally affects children and young people.

● Children are particularly vulnerable to ill-treatment by those more powerful than they are.

● To focus now on protecting the rights and interests of children is to invest in the future.

A 'Children's Rights Commissioner'

These problems could be tackled by creating an independent and wide-ranging statutory office to promote the rights and interests of children and young people. It is not the only measure which should be taken but it would be a unique and highly effective contribution.

■3. A Proposal for a Children's Rights Commissioner

This section describes in detail the proposed features for the Commissioner and his/her staff. Some are adapted from aspects of other independent public bodies.

Mission

The purpose of the Commissioner would be to promote children's rights throughout the UK, by:

(i) influencing policy makers and practitioners to take greater account of children's rights and interests;

(ii) promoting compliance with the minimum standards set by the United Nations Convention on the Rights of the Child and other relevant international treaties or agreements;

(iii) seeking to ensure that children have effective means of redress when their rights are disregarded.

(Children are defined as anyone under eighteen.)

Guiding principles

● A key statement of principles to guide the Commissioner would be the UN Convention, an extensive document providing internationally recognised standards for children's rights (see appendix 5). This and other international agreements would provide a baseline of minimum standards, but the Commissioner would advocate further rights in the context of the UK.

● Although established by government, the Commissioner would be independent in action and policy stances from government and all other bodies.

● The Commissioner would adopt a broad perspective cutting across departments and agencies.

● The Commissioner would consistently seek input into his/her work from children and young people, and would co-operate closely with other organisations working for children and young people.

Activities

The Commissioner would have the following main functions:

● The Commissioner would highlight ways in which current policies or practices fail to respect the rights and interests of children and young people, and propose measures to rectify this. S/he would have the power to examine, report on and issue recommendations on any area of policy or practice affecting children and young people. The possible scope of the Commissioner's work would cover central government, local government, public agencies, voluntary organisations, private bodies and international developments, but government policy would be at the core. Those who are subject to recommendations from the Commissioner would be legally bound to give them full consideration and respond within a fixed period.

● The Commissioner would have the power to conduct formal investigations.

● The Commissioner would analyse and comment on proposed new government policies in terms of their likely impact on children and young people. In certain circumstances ministers would be required to consult the Commissioner, and the Commissioner could also ask government departments to produce 'child impact statements' about their proposals.

● The Commissioner could publish information about children and young people and their rights, and conduct or commission research linked to policy development.

● The Commissioner would possess powers to monitor children's use of complaints procedures, and would press for their extension and improvement. S/he would produce a code of good practice (see appendix 4). The Commissioner would not deal with individual complaints. A separate independent body could be provided for receiving complaints from children in care. Children and young people have access to many complaints procedures. But there are serious gaps and inadequacies, and the use by children and young people of existing procedures is very limited (see appendix 3).

● In cases which raise important questions of principle the Commissioner would be able to assist legal action taken by children or participate in legal proceedings in his/her own name on behalf of children's interests.

Structure and ways of working

● Further consultation is necessary on the best means of operation in Wales, Scotland and Northern Ireland.

● A Parliamentary Select Committee relating to the Commissioner's activities should be set up.

● The Commissioner would establish mechanisms for direct input into his/her work from children and young people.

● The Commissioner would also establish mechanisms for regular discussion of his/her activities with voluntary bodies and other organisations.

(This part of the report also covers reporting arrangements, staffing and funding, and method of appointment.)

Creating the Commissioner

Legislation will be required to establish the Commissioner. (See section 4 for a framework for the legislation.)

Conclusion

Creating a Children's Rights Commissioner would be an important reform for the UK's 13.2 million children and young people. Its work would improve law, policy and practice affecting children and young people; raise the status of children and young people in policy-making; and ensure that politicians, policy-makers and practitioners take children's rights and interests more seriously. Policy affecting children would take more account of children's rights and interests and the need for co-ordination, and would be based on a better understanding of its impact on children and young people and their perspective. The Commissioner's work would also result in better systems for children who are victims of injustice to obtain redress, and in less ill-treatment. Finally it would help the UK fulfil its obligations under the UN Convention on the Rights of the Child.

Introduction

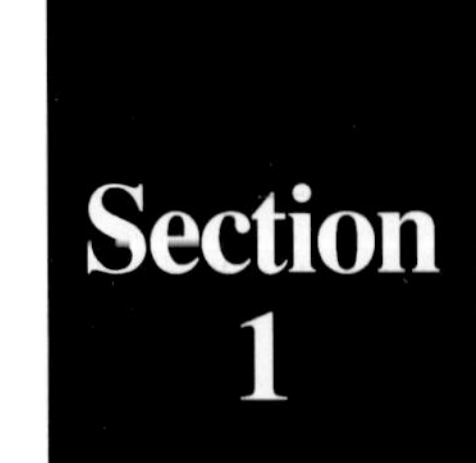

'The well-being of children requires political action at the highest level. We are determined to take that action. We ourselves make a solemn commitment to give high priority to the rights of children.'[1]

So said the leaders of the world's nations at the World Summit for Children held in September 1990 at the United Nations in New York, the largest gathering of world leaders in history. 71 heads of state and government (including Margaret Thatcher) and other leading politicians gathered to pledge themselves to improve the lives of children in their own countries and throughout the globe.

The World Summit and the United Nations Convention on the Rights of the Child (which was adopted in 1989) have both served to raise the profile of children's rights internationally, although it will be some time before the children of the world discover the extent to which promises are translated into action. Children's rights have also received more attention in the UK in the past few years, and this has resulted in change for the better, including in particular the Children Act 1989 which extends the rights of children and young people in England and Wales in family law, child protection and other areas. This report proposes a measure which would be a further major contribution to children's rights in the UK: the creation of a 'Children's Rights Commissioner' - an independent statutory office aimed at promoting children's rights and interests.

Like the UN Convention on the Rights of the Child, we use the term 'children's rights' in a wide-ranging sense. It includes the right to be protected from abuse, the right to suitable education and health services, the right to live without poverty, the right to safe play areas, the right to participate in decisions, the right to have your interests taken into account, the right to have people look at things from your point of view: in short, how society should treat children and young people.

In the past 20 years or so many people concerned about children and young people have recognised the need for greater representation of their rights and interests at a national level. A variety of possible remedies have been suggested, few of which have been implemented (see appendix 1). Most of the proposals have been lacking in specifics. The Calouste Gulbenkian Foundation commissioned this report to examine in detail the idea of creating an independent governmental office to represent children's interests and to produce a detailed and practical blueprint for such an institution.

As part of our work we circulated an initial outline of our thinking to a wide range of children's and young people's organisations, professional bodies, and other interested groups. The response was overwhelmingly positive and enthusiastic, as well as containing many useful and constructive comments. It is clear that many children's organisations and other bodies involved in the field would welcome the creation of the kind of institution we are proposing.

During the course of our work the Scottish Child Care Law Review Group, a multi-disciplinary group set up by the Secretary of State for Scotland to recommend improvements in child care law, raised the idea of creating a 'Child Welfare Commission'[2]. Although described in much less detail, this would have a remit and some functions similar to those of the Children's Rights Commissioner we are proposing (see appendix 1 for further details). Since such a Commission would not be limited to child care law, it was outside the terms of reference of the Scottish Group to consider the idea in detail. But they said 'it represents an important idea ... with significant potential for improving the welfare of children' and recommended that: 'A separate examination should be commissioned by the Secretary of State of the case for and the feasibility of a Child Welfare Commission in Scotland'.

The Secretary of State for Scotland invited relevant organisations to comment on the Review Group's report by December 1990. The responses[3] show there was virtually unanimous backing - including from children's organisations, regional councils, children's panels, health boards and professional bodies - for the idea of further examining the possibility of a Child Welfare Commission. Points stressed in several replies were the need for the Commission to cover all policy areas affecting children and the advantages of it helping to monitor the implementation of the United Nations Convention on the Rights of the Child. The Scottish Secretary is now (March 1991) considering what action to take.

It is not only in the UK that support is growing for establishing independent public bodies to promote children's rights. The idea has been a consistent theme amongst campaigners for children's rights in many parts of the world in the past decade or so. Some countries have already taken action and UNICEF is seeking to promote the concept internationally. The world leader was Norway which created the post of *Barneombud* or Children's Ombudsperson in 1981. Since then New Zealand has appointed a Commissioner for Children, and in other countries similar posts have been created at a regional or local level. The Council of Europe is currently considering the best mechanisms for promoting children's rights in its member states. For more details of international developments see appendix 2.

Creating a Children's Rights Commissioner would be in line with national and international trends towards greater recognition of children's rights. Of course a variety of measures are needed to assist children and young people, but whether or not other improvements are introduced, the existence of such a Commissioner would achieve a great deal. We hope that this report will be widely discussed and will lead to the creation of an institution which in the words of the World Summit's declaration will ensure the UK gives 'high priority to the rights of children'.

Section 2 of the report explains the need for a Children's Rights Commissioner. Section 3 contains the detailed proposal for one. Section 4 lists points which would have to be covered in legislation creating the Commissioner. Background information is contained in a number of appendices. Appendix 1 summarises previous proposals for improving the representation of children's rights and interests in the UK. Appendix 2 describes independent public bodies which exist to promote children's rights in other countries. Appendix 3 details complaints procedures available to children and young people. Appendix 4 lists principles of good practice for the use of complaints procedures by children and young people. Appendix 5 contains the United Nations Convention on the Rights of the Child.

Notes

1. World Summit for Children Declaration, 30 September, 1990
2. *Review of Child Care Law in Scotland*, Report of a Review Group appointed by the Secretary of State, HMSO, 1990
3. Made available to us by the Scottish Office Library

The Need for a Children's Rights Commissioner

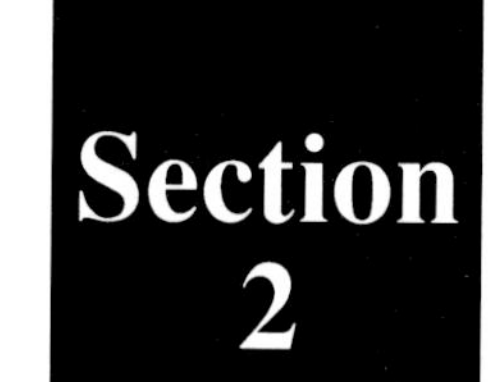

As noted in the previous section and appendix 1, many possibilities have been suggested for creating some kind of governmental or public body in the UK to promote the rights and interests of children and young people: the Children's Committee, a Minister or Ministry for children, a permanent Cabinet Committee on children, a children's 'ombudsperson', a House of Commons Select Committee, a Child Welfare Commission, etc. All these ideas have stemmed from a deep-seated and widespread concern that current policy-making and practice in areas which affect children often do not give enough recognition to their rights and interests, and that some institutional change is needed to rectify this. Why is it necessary to create such an institution specifically for the benefit of children and young people? And what sort of institution would be effective?

1. The Need for Action

A. The UN Convention

The United Nations Convention on the Rights of the Child, which the UK has pledged that it will ratify (March 1991), will provide the Government with a wide range of new obligations towards children and young people. (See appendix 5 for its text.) A forthcoming handbook[1] by one of us, Peter Newell, demonstrates that the UK still has a considerable way to go in satisfying many articles of the Convention. Furthermore Article 4 of the Convention requires states to 'undertake all appropriate legislative, administrative, and other measures,.for the implementation of the rights recognised in the present Convention'. And under Article 42, states must 'make the principles and provisions of the Convention widely known, by appropriate and active means, to adults and children alike'.

The Government must respond to the requirements of the Convention. It needs to discharge the responsibilities imposed by the Convention, take action to ensure that the Convention is well-publicised and implemented on a long-term basis, and also make sure that children's rights receive the political priority they are entitled to and which the Convention is meant to guarantee. (The Council of Europe is considering mechanisms which could be established at international and national levels to promote children's rights (see appendix 2): an imaginative and exciting decision by the UK could provide an influential model which others in Europe - and further afield - might adopt.)

B. The political process and decision-making

Our democracy is based on the premise that groups of people will stand up for their own interests and rights, but generally speaking children and young people are not in a position to do this. Children are a large but uniquely uninfluential sector of the population. They are particularly powerless and vulnerable, and are generally highly restricted in both the extent to which they can take decisions about their own lives and the extent to which they can participate in society's overall decision-making processes. (Of course as children get older they gradually acquire more control over their own lives. The definition we use for children is anyone under 18, since that is the legal definition, and it is also the one used in the UN Convention. But even though 17 year olds have more say over their own lives than younger people do, they are still excluded from the democratic process.)

The UK's 13.2 million under-18s constitute 23% of the population but they do not have a say in who runs the country. Children and young people under 18 cannot vote, they cannot stand to be MPs or local councillors, they do not hold high offices in political parties or in other important institutions, they are very rarely involved in consultative exercises undertaken by decision-making bodies: in other words they do not play a part in the political process which determines both nationally and locally the policies that affect their lives. These policies are determined by adults. This is a crucial difference between children and other groups of people who face discrimination: they are generally unable to organise themselves to put direct pressure on politicians through the ordinary political process.

Politicians are under pressure to devise and present policies in a way which reflects the self-interest of various constituent groups of adults ranging from war widows to farmers and from mortgage-payers to commuters: they are not under the same degree of pressure with regard to children and young people. As a result the impact of policies on children and young people receives less care and attention. Children may be the subjects of a fair amount of political rhetoric, but unfortunately the rhetoric tends to be empty and unconnected to practical policies.

Many adults (especially of course parents) are concerned about children and young people, and raise their voices in support of making society better for them. Many professionals have the welfare of children and young people as their concern. And many children's organisations do valuable work lobbying and campaigning for children's rights. But these organisations would be the first to say that despite the political efforts some adults make on behalf of children and young people, their concerns are a very low political priority and the political process tends to see the issues involved from an adult rather than a child perspective.

Children and young people are not only cut off from law-making and policy-making, they also often cannot fully participate in decisions about practice which directly affect them. For example, while some schools have school councils and other ways of involving pupils, many schools have no means for incorporating them in decision-making. Similarly, while legally children and young people in care must be consulted about decisions which affect their lives, they are often excluded from the case conferences or other meetings where the crucial decisions are actually taken.

To summarise, children are a very low political priority; often when issues affecting them are considered they are not looked at from a child's perspective; and often even when they are, children's rights are not taken seriously.

What are the practical consequences of all this? We do not have the space here for an account of how children and young people have often been badly served in practice by many aspects of law and policy: examples have been documented thoroughly elsewhere[2]. The problems are extensive and range over all areas of policy: from the continuing lack of a children's perspective in much child protection work, to the high number of children killed in road accidents; from the lack of high quality provision for under-fives, to many housing estates' unsuitability and shortage of facilities for children; and from the high levels of disaffection and drop-out rates in education, to the lack of power over their own lives experienced by many children and young people in care.

C. Co-ordination

Another factor which adversely influences policy-making affecting children and young people, at both central and local government level, is the wide dispersal of responsibilities.

At central government level responsibilities which affect children and young people are distributed across the following departments[3]:

Department of Education and Science (education, the youth service);
Department of Employment (training, employment, the careers service);
Department of the Environment (out of school sport);
Department of Health (health services, social services, child abuse, adoption, regulation of day care, nutrition, care and protection of children, treatment of juvenile delinquents);
Home Office (criminal justice, magistrates' courts proceedings involving custody and maintenance of children);
Lord Chancellor's Department (family law);
Department of Social Security (social security).
In Wales, Scotland and Northern Ireland, some of the functions above are carried out by the Welsh, Scottish and Northern Ireland Offices.

These wide divisions of responsibility are replicated at local level between the various local authority departments, health authorities, etc. Lack of co-ordination has been criticised by a number of official reports on children's services. And child abuse inquiries in particular have condemned failures of co-operation between social services, health services, the police, the NSPCC, education welfare services, etc. (Recent government guidance[4] has attempted to deal with this problem.) The under-fives and 16-19 year olds are two age groups particularly affected by split responsibility for services.

Given that in the UK government and local authority departments are divided on functional lines, it is inevitable that for a specific group of people such as children and young people, responsibilities for different aspects of their lives will be dispersed. It is also true that some mechanisms to co-ordinate policy have been established: for example, at central government level there are official inter-departmental co-ordinating committees on juvenile delinquency, child abuse and services for pre-school children[5]. But nevertheless there is no one in government with the authority to look across the board at how policy generally affects children and young people. And while this applies to many other groups of people too, the low political priority given to children and the comparable ease with which their concerns are ignored make it a more serious problem.

It should be noted that government has established mechanisms to improve policy co-ordination in some other areas, eg the creation of a Minister for the Disabled, and the Ministerial Group on Women which was set up in 1986 to provide a co-ordinated examination of policy issues of special concern to women. And in September 1990 the government announced there would be a nominated minister in each department responsible for considering the environmental implications of all that department's policies[6]. (It is also worth noting that some other groups of people already have national statutory bodies which promote their rights: the Commission for Racial Equality combats race discrimination, the Equal Opportunities Commission combats sex discrimination, and the Mental Health Act Commission promotes the rights of detained mental patients.)

D. Children's vulnerability

Children are particularly vulnerable to ill-treatment by those more powerful than they are for a number of reasons: their physical weakness, their inexperience and lack of understanding, their lack of independence and their control by adults, their restricted opportunities to take action on their own behalf, the tendency of many adults not to listen to them or take their complaints seriously, and the compulsion they are under to attend particular institutions (as well as compulsory schooling, over 200,000 children are forced to live for all or much of their childhood in various kinds of residential institutions). Several scandals in children's homes, boarding schools and elsewhere which have recently come to light have provided particularly disturbing illustrations of the consequences for some children of this vulnerability, but there are also many less serious grievances which should nevertheless be examined and put right.

Therefore it is particularly necessary that children and young people have effective complaints procedures in the case of ill-treatment, which should both help to provide suitable remedies and prevent ill-treatment in the first place. This is an important part of promoting children's rights. (See appendices 3 and 4 for information on existing complaints procedures, their use by children and young people, and a possible code of good practice.)

E. Investing in the future

Children are the country's future, and what happens to them now will determine their abilities and attitudes as adults and the nature of our country - and the world - from now on. To focus on protecting the rights and interests of children is a way of investing in the future. The increasing political priority attached to environmental issues reflects a similar concern to ensure that current generations do not jeopardise the welfare of future ones.

Furthermore, because they are still growing and developing, children are more sensitive - both physically and psychologically - to the conditions they and their families live in. They are more susceptible to the harmful consequences of pollution, poverty, homelessness, etc. This emphasises the need to adopt policies now which provide properly for the future of our society.

2. A 'Children's Rights Commissioner'

The problems just described could be tackled by creating an independent and wide-ranging statutory office, with powers and duties laid down in law, to promote the rights and interests of children and young people.

Being independent it would be free to act as it sees fit in the cause of children and young people without having to comply with external pressures. With a wide-ranging remit it would be able to cover any area of policy or practice affecting children and young people and take an overall perspective. And as a statutory body, it would have the following important features: it is likely to have a high public profile; it would have clout in government circles and with local authorities and other organisations; and it could have specific legal powers (eg to require responses to recommendations, to hold investigations: see next section) which could only be granted to a statutory body.

This is not the only measure which could and should be taken in response to the need for action outlined above. But it would be a unique and highly effective contribution. It would also fit with (but is not dependent on) many of the other proposals that have been made for increasing representation of children's interests, for example the creation of a Minister for Children. In fact, were such a Minister established, we would expect that they would work together closely and productively (although not always in agreement - since the Minister would be committed to government policy). Similarly it could fit well with various further voluntary sector initiatives, making different contributions and mutually strengthening each other's work. (This includes the current (March 1991) proposal to set up a voluntary sector 'Children's Rights Development Unit' to promote implementation of the UN Convention. The Unit is planned as a three-year project working collaboratively with a wide range of organisations committed to the Convention's principles.)

We propose that the office we are suggesting should be called the 'Children's Rights Commissioner' or 'Children's Commissioner'. We favour a Commissioner with staff rather than a Commission because this would help promote a better public profile and be more efficient, flexible, decisive and dynamic. The next section gives full details of the proposal.

Notes

1. To be published by the National Children's Bureau in collaboration with the Gulbenkian Foundation (summer 1991)
2. For sources which cover a wide range of topics see for example: Jonathan Bradshaw's recent report *Child Poverty and Deprivation in the UK*, published by the National Children's Bureau; Peter Newell's forthcoming handbook on how the UK measures up to the UN Convention on the Rights of the Child; the annual *Children in Danger Factfile* produced by National Children's Home; and issues of the Children's Legal Centre's magazine *Childright*. There are of course many reports, books and articles covering particular issues affecting children and young people.
3. *Hansard*, 25 October, 1990 col 276/7
4. For example, *Working together for the protection of children from abuse* (Local authority circular 88/10), issued by the Department of Health and Social Security in 1988. This is currently (March 1991) under review.
5. *Hansard*, 25 October, 1990, col 277
6. *This Common Inheritance - Britain's Environmental Strategy*, Government White Paper, Cm 1200, HMSO, p230

A Proposal for a Children's Rights Commissioner

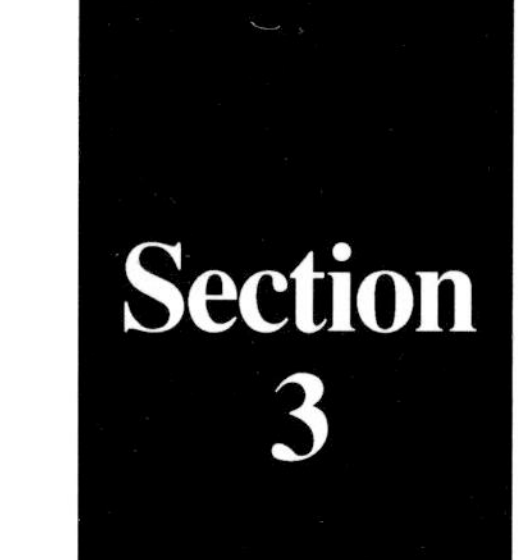

This section describes in detail the proposed features for an independent statutory office - a Children's Rights Commissioner with staff - to promote the rights of children and young people under 18 in the UK.

The features proposed stem from the analysis in the previous section of why a Children's Rights Commissioner is needed, and also from examination of the constitution and activities of many other independent or semi-independent public offices which influence the policy of central government, local authorities and other bodies, help individuals obtain redress for grievances, or have similar responsibilities.

The offices we have looked at include the Commissioners for Local Administration in England, Wales and Scotland, and the Northern Ireland Commissioner for Complaints, the Parliamentary Commissioner for Administration, the Commission for Racial Equality, the Equal Opportunities Commission, the Chief Inspector of Prisons, the Social Services Inspectorate (England), the Official Solicitor's Department, the National Consumer Council, the Council on Tribunals, the Law Commission, the Audit Commission, the National Audit Office, the Data Protection Registrar, the Police Complaints Authority, the Mental Health Act Commission, the Social Security Advisory Committee and the Legal Services Ombudsman.

1. Mission

The 'mission' or fundamental purpose of the Children's Rights Commissioner would be to promote children's rights throughout the UK (see below under 'Structure and ways of working' for further discussion of Wales, Scotland and Northern Ireland). This would be done by:

(i) influencing policy-makers and practitioners to take greater account of children's rights and interests;

(ii) promoting compliance with the minimum standards set by the United Nations Convention on the Rights of the Child and other relevant international treaties or agreements;

(iii) seeking to ensure that children have effective means of redress when their rights are disregarded.

(Children are defined as anyone from birth and under eighteen.)

2. Guiding Principles

A. International conventions

The Commissioner would promote the principles laid down in the United Nations Convention on the Rights of the Child (which would be contained in a Schedule to the Act establishing the Commissioner). The Commissioner would encourage the government and others to comply with the Convention. The text of the Convention is in appendix 5.

Since its approval by the United Nations General Assembly in November 1989 the Convention on the Rights of the Child has provided internationally recognised standards. At the time of writing (March 1991), 75 states have agreed to implement the Convention by ratifying it, and the number is growing rapidly. The British Government has signed the Convention, which indicates support in principle, but has not yet ratified, although it has stated its intention to do so following detailed consideration of its implications. (The text added to the Commissioner's Act as a Schedule would have to reflect any reservations about the Convention made by the UK. However this would only represent *minimum* standards for the Commissioner to promote.)

The UN Convention, which was drawn up over a ten year period, is extensive and detailed. It adds distinctive and necessary rights for children and young people to other rights already protected in international conventions. It encompasses civil and political rights as well as economic and social rights, and the issues covered range from access to education, health services and social security, to freedom of expression and association.

A central principle for the Commissioner's work is stated by Article 3: 'In all actions concerning children, whether undertaken by public or private social welfare institutions, courts of law, administrative authorities or legislative bodies, the best interests of the child shall be a primary consideration'. So linking the Commissioner to the UN Convention means that the Commissioner will be promoting the right of children and young people to have their interests properly considered in decision-making at all levels.

Other key Articles include Article 12 which lays down the right of children to have their views taken into account in decisions which affect them; and Article 2 which insists that the rights in the Convention must be protected without discrimination on any ground including race, sex or disability.

Given the status and range of the Convention it should provide a key statement of principles to guide the Commissioner. This ensures that the Commissioner's actions are founded on a clear body of principles rather than just an individual interpretation of children's rights. The Commissioner's standing would also benefit from being connected to a statement of children's rights which has such authority. And this connection could also help the government, through support for the Commissioner, to discharge its duties, once it has ratified the Convention, to publicise it (under Article 42) and ensure its implementation (Article 4).

The Commissioner would also be guided by the other international treaties or agreements signed by the UK which apply specifically to children and young people or lay down rights which apply to children as much as to adults. These include the European Convention on Human Rights; the International Covenant on Civil and Political Rights; the International Covenant on Economic, Social and Cultural Rights; the Council of Europe Social Charter; and the United Nations Standard Minimum Rules for the Administration of Juvenile Justice. (The Council of Europe is also considering drawing up a European treaty on children's rights - see appendix 2.)

Although the UN Convention is the most comprehensive document, there are points where other Conventions the UK has accepted provide more extensive rights. The UN Convention itself says (Article 41) that nothing it contains should undermine 'any provisions which are more conducive to the realisation of the rights of the child' which are contained in a state's law or other international agreements in force for that state.

In promoting the rights of children and young people the Commissioner would not be limited to those laid down in these international agreements, but would advocate further rights that s/he felt were necessary or beneficial in the context of the UK. The international agreements only provide a baseline of minimum standards.

B. National law

The Commissioner's views on policy would also be guided by some important tenets of national law affecting children. For example, the House of Lords in the *Gillick* case decided that (except where otherwise laid down by statute) children have the right to take decisions for themselves when they have sufficient understanding. (In Scotland the Commissioner would need to take into account the rights currently accorded to 'minors' - girls over 12 and boys over 14.) Another important principle is stipulated in the Children Act 1989 which states[1] (in the context of court proceedings) that delays in determining questions relating to a child are likely to prejudice the child's welfare. They should therefore be avoided.

C. Independence

Although established by government, the Commissioner would be independent in action from government and all other bodies, and would be entirely free to determine his/her policy stances and activities (within the law setting out his/her legal powers and duties). The Commissioner's effectiveness will of course depend on using this independence to develop productive relationships with ministers and others.

D. Width of perspective

The Commissioner would adopt a broad overview of the responsibilities for children of various departments and agencies. His/her actions would thus stem from an overall assessment of how policies impact on children and young people. The Commissioner would encourage co-ordination throughout government departments, local authority departments, other public agencies and the voluntary sector.

E. Working with children and young people and with other bodies

The Commissioner would consistently seek input into his/her work from children and young people. S/he would also co-operate closely and exchange information with other organisations working for children and young people, including voluntary bodies. (See subsections 4E and F below.) In particular the Commissioner should take care to avoid duplicating work already being done effectively by others. The Commissioner would also when appropriate work with other independent public bodies such as the Commission for Racial Equality, the Equal Opportunities Commission and others listed above in the introduction to this section.

3. Activities

To pursue the aims stated above the Commissioner would have a range of functions and would need the legal powers necessary to carry them out. The functions include the following: reporting on any area of policy and practice affecting children and making recommendations; conducting investigations; being consulted by government on proposed new policy; publishing information and conducting research; reviewing complaints procedures; and initiating or assisting with legal action.

A. Influencing policy and practice

(i) Reports, recommendations, etc

A key part of the Commissioner's role would be to identify and highlight ways in which current policies or practices fail to respect the rights and interests of children and young people and to propose measures to rectify this.

The Commissioner would therefore have the power to examine, report on and issue recommendations on any area of policy or practice affecting children and young people. The Commissioner would both be concerned with policy intentions and how those policies are implemented in practice.

The scope of the Commissioner's work would cover the policies and activities of central government, local government, public agencies, voluntary organisations (including child welfare organisations) and private bodies such as employers or independent schools, as well as European and international developments which affect the UK. S/he could also focus on the inter-relationship between any of these bodies. The Commissioner must have the right to tackle any issue within any of these fields which s/he feels is of sufficient importance for children and young people, but of course s/he could only be active on a limited number of topics at any one time. The Commissioner could make recommendations aimed at specific bodies or could issue general guidance. However since central government sets the parameters within which everyone else operates, government policy will undoubtedly be at the core of the Commissioner's work.

The Commissioner would publish his/her reports with their recommendations (as well as an annual report - see subsection 4B below). They would be circulated to appropriate government, local government and other bodies, and would be available to the public. S/he could also issue advisory codes of practice - these could first be issued in draft form for consultation with appropriate organisations. Some codes of practice could cover how the principles of the UN Convention should be put into effect.

Legislation would have to ensure that those who are subject to specific recommendations from the Commissioner (including ministers) give them proper consideration. They would have to consider the Commissioner's report and have regard to his/her recommendations. They would also have to respond to the Commissioner within a specified period (say three months unless the Commissioner allows a longer time) stating what action they have taken or intend to take in the light of the recommendations. If they intend not to comply (either partly or wholly) with any of the recommendations they would have to state their reasons publicly. It will be important for the Commissioner to follow up recommendations persistently and devote enough effort to monitoring their implementation, if necessary over quite long periods. The Commissioner would have the right, say for a five year period after his/her recommendations were made, to require reports on progress towards their implementation.

In some circumstances the Commissioner may conclude the UN Convention as ratified by the UK is not being implemented by a particular body or bodies. In this case the Commissioner could issue a 'compliance notice' which would give details of the failure and state how in the Commissioner's opinion it should be remedied. The law on responding to the Commissioner's recommendations would also apply to compliance notices. In these cases the Commissioner could also be given the power, where the body involved still fails to comply, to have this fact publicised (eg in national or local newspapers) at the body's expense - this is similar to the recently extended powers of the Commissioners for Local Administration[2] and those of the new Legal Services Ombudsman[3]. The Commissioner would maintain a public register of compliance notices. (Since the Convention will not have the force of law in the UK - as an international treaty it ties the government to ensure it is implemented within its territory rather than directly binding individual bodies within the UK - the Commissioner cannot enforce it directly.)

As an independent office the Commissioner would not be part of the government's decision-making apparatus or that of any other body and could not therefore have direct control over any area of policy and decisions concerning children and young people. This independence is essential for the Commissioner to undertake - and be seen by others to undertake - a disinterested scrutiny of all aspects of the government's and other bodies' policy and activity affecting children. (We refer elsewhere (see section 2 and appendix 1) to the separate proposals that have been made for a Minister for Children, the creation of which would be compatible with the existence of a Children's Rights Commissioner.)

Constitutionally decisions within the responsibilities of central and local government must in the end be taken by elected ministers or councillors who are accountable to voters. They should not be overridden by unelected officials (although of course the courts may intervene if they act against their legal duties or outside their legal powers). Therefore fundamental constitutional principles require that the Commissioner's policy recommendations could not be binding on elected bodies concerned.

In any case the introduction of binding recommendations from the Commissioner would almost certainly lead to an appeals process and legal actions from bodies reluctant to comply. This would be time-consuming and would increase the staffing and budget (especially for legal cases) which the Commissioner required. In these cases the implementation of the recommendations would also be subject to delays and the risk of being overturned. Organisations may also be less co-operative and open with the Commissioner in discussing policy if they think that later on they are going to be doing battle in court. Neither the Commission for Local Administration in England, Wales and Scotland, nor the Health Service Commissioner, for example, can issue binding recommendations. (Of course legal action could be instituted in circumstances where it was found that the law was being broken.)

It is essential that the Commissioner is not primarily reactive but is free to choose the areas s/he reports on and can act on his/her own initiative in the light of his/her own priorities. The likely criteria used to define priority issues could include the following: the number of children and young people affected; the seriousness of the way in which they are affected; whether those affected are also disadvantaged in other ways; the extent to which the issue has been raised already or is being raised by others; the likelihood of achieving positive change; and the possible 'knock-on' effects for other situations.

Some of the Commissioner's time would be spent on responding to requests for his/her views from other bodies, whether specific invitations or as a part of normal open consultative exercises. The Commissioner could be asked by ministers to examine and report on particular areas of policy, and would normally comply. (However since several government departments have responsibility for children's matters, the Commissioner could receive requests from a number of different departments and it would need to be within the Commissioner's discretion to decline.) See (iii) below for procedures for the government to consult the Commissioner on proposed new policy.

(ii) Investigations

Like other similar bodies the Commissioner would need wide formal powers to launch investigations in furtherance of his/her duties, including powers to require access to records and documents and also to question individuals. The ability to launch formal investigations would ensure the Commissioner had access to objective evidence which may be needed to discover and demonstrate denials of the rights and interests of children. Investigations could be held into the policy and practice of one body or of a number of connected or similar bodies. The Commissioner would be required to give proper notice of the investigation and its purpose to those concerned, and there would be guarantees of confidentiality for information supplied where appropriate. A report containing any recommendations for action would be issued after the investigation.

The Commissioner may have to consult with other bodies with investigatory powers or responsibilities such as the Commissioners for Local Administration, the Social Services Inspectorate, the Commission for Racial Equality and the Equal Opportunities Commission to ensure overlapping or conflicting investigations are avoided. (Joint investigations into issues of mutual concern could be considered but may pose difficulties because of the different legal requirements governing other organisations' powers to hold investigations.)

(iii) Influencing proposed new Government policy

It is better to influence policy while it is being conceived rather than after it has been put into practice. The best way to ensure that new legislation takes into account the rights and interests of children and young people would be for the department involved to consult the Commissioner at an early stage (and certainly before instructions are given to Parliamentary Counsel, who draft government Bills). The Commissioner would analyse and comment on proposed new policies in terms of their likely impact on children and young people. We hope that on the basis of its expertise the Commissioner's office would build up close informal links with civil servants in all relevant government departments.

Whenever ministers intend to amend or repeal specified major pieces of legislation affecting children they should be obliged to consult the Commissioner at an early stage. The Commissioner would then have a duty to consider and respond to the points raised. This would apply for example to the Children Act 1989, major Education Acts, the Adoption Act 1976 and the Children and Young Persons Act 1933. A full list of such Acts would be spelt out in a schedule to the Act establishing the Commissioner and this could be added to (but not subtracted from) by order. This consultation requirement would also be included in appropriate Acts passed in future. A similar requirement would apply to the making or repealing of statutory instruments under specified sections of specified Acts. (The requirement on ministers to consult the Commissioner would also apply when they have to consider how to respond to private members' legislation attempting to alter the specified Acts.) The Commissioner could issue a dispensation from the requirement to consult for changes which are technical or unimportant.

Each government department should also have a Code of Consultation containing advice to consult the Commissioner at an early stage on certain proposals which would impact particularly on children or affect children differently from the way adults would be affected. The Code could also say that departments should inform the Commissioner when they start work on a relevant new issue. The text of the Code and the exact criteria for the proposals involved would be agreed between the Commissioner and each department, or possibly one Code would be agreed between the Commissioner and the lead department relating to him/her and be circulated to other departments. The extent of the Commissioner's ability to comment would have to depend on his/her resources at the time. (A Code like this already exists for the Council on Tribunals[4] - it is agreed with the Lord Chancellor's Department and applies to all departments.)

Most government departments do not have children and young people at the centre of their concerns. For the reasons given in section 2, a mechanism is needed to ensure that they fully consider the interests of children when making policy. The Commissioner should therefore have the power to require government departments to issue a 'child impact statement' to accompany White Papers, Green Papers, Bills etc. This would indicate the likely impact on children and young people. It would always be public. The Commissioner could also request a child impact statement on for example the budget, the autumn statement on public spending or the annual public spending White Paper. (It would of course be unrealistic to expect the Chancellor to consult the Commissioner on a budget prior to the budget speech, but this would be a way of applying a children's perspective to one of the government's most important annual events.) A blanket requirement to issue child impact statements on all policy proposals would probably be treated as a formality to be observed in a minimal way and would devalue the concept.

The departments most likely to be required to provide child impact statements are not those where the impact of decisions on children is at the forefront of discussion eg the Department of Health, the Department of Education and Science or the Lord Chancellor's Department's Family Law Division. Rather it is those whose policies impact on both children and adults, and where the impact on children may not have received sufficient attention. The process of requiring child impact statements could also help promote co-ordination between different departments since statements they issue would be compared. It would also encourage departments to ensure they have consulted the Commissioner properly at earlier stages. Departments would be obliged to respond to comments the Commissioner makes on a child impact statement.

Aside from statutory requirements for consultation on changes to specified Acts, the procedures laid down in a Code of Consultation, and the child impact statement process, the Commissioner could also as s/he thinks fit comment to ministers on Bills, White Papers, Green Papers, and other proposals.

B. Information and research

The Commissioner would be able to do the following:

- publish and distribute information about children and young people and their rights (but the Commissioner would avoid duplicating material already published by others);
- conduct or commission research (we envisage the Commissioner would rarely if at all conduct original field research given the range of bodies already involved in research concerning children and young people, but s/he may wish to conduct or commission applied research closely linked to the development of policies);
- review the government's collection of statistics concerning children and young people and report on gaps, inadequacies and possible improvements (but the Commissioner would not be directly involved in collecting statistics). This would be useful because attention has often been drawn to the need for more comprehensive and consistent sets of statistics about children in the UK[5].

C. Complaints

Part of the Commissioner's role would be to seek to ensure that children and young people under 18 throughout the UK have effective means of redress when their rights are disregarded.

This is a necessary part of the Commissioner's role of promoting policies which protect children's rights. Any body which has responsibilities affecting children and young people needs to have adequate processes for dealing with cases where the rights of individuals may have been infringed. The Commissioner would monitor complaints procedures to see that they are operating properly and in all relevant fields. And of course the Commissioner's wider work should have the effect of empowering children and young people and reducing infringements of their rights in the first place.

(i) Complaints procedures

Children and young people already have access to many complaints procedures. Current developments, including implementation of the Children Act 1989, will expand those provided by local authorities. There are also the Commissioners for Local Administration and complaints procedures provided by various statutory, voluntary, private and professional bodies. (Appendix 3 provides details of complaints procedures available to children and young people.) However, there are serious inadequacies and gaps. Furthermore it is clear from the research for this report (see appendix 3) that the use by children and young people of existing procedures is very limited.

An important task for the Commissioner would be to review the full range of services used by children and young people and existing complaints procedures available to them to reveal gaps and inadequacies. In particular the Commissioner would wish to ensure they are comprehensive, well-publicised, accessible, speedy and effective. The Commissioner could produce a code of good practice for complaints procedures - see appendix 4 for an indication of points it might contain. The Commissioner would need to pay particular attention to procedures for children who are in the most vulnerable circumstances eg children in care or children living in various institutions such as hospitals, young offender institutions or boarding schools.

The Commissioner would have the power to receive information about and report on complaints made (and their outcomes) to the full range of statutory complaints procedures (see appendix 3) by under-18s or those acting on their behalf. The Commissioner would not be able to review individual decisions on complaints. While it may not be possible to require those running complaints procedures in the voluntary and private sectors to provide the Commissioner with similar information, it should be possible to negotiate voluntary agreements. The rights of individuals to confidentiality would of course be respected. This information would enable the Commissioner to assess how complaints are handled and whether their outcomes are satisfactory. It would also provide him/her with invaluable data on the concerns of children and young people which would be useful in formulating policies in his/her wider role of promoting children's rights.

Legislation governing statutory complaints procedures (eg the Children Act 1989, the Education Reform Act 1988) should be amended to ensure that those running them have a duty to 'have regard to' advice provided by the Commissioner.

It is already clear that some extensions in statutory procedures are necessary. For example, it is likely that the Commissioner would press for the following:

a) extending the powers of the Commissioners for Local Administration, eg to cover internal school matters and to allow them to initiate an investigation without having received a complaint (the Local Commissioners have themselves pressed for these changes);

b) extending the remit of the Mental Health Act Commission to cover 'informal' patients - most children in mental hospitals are informal patients admitted by their parents, and only the few detained under the Mental Health Act come under the Commission (the Commission has itself sought this change);

c) requiring local education authorities (and governing bodies of grant-maintained schools and proprietors of independent schools and non-maintained special schools) to set up comprehensive complaints procedures for pupils. (Under the Education Reform Act 1988 LEAs need only have procedures for complaints about the curriculum. Under the Children Act 1989 independent schools with boarding accommodation for less than 50 pupils will have to have a complaints procedure because they will also have to register as children's homes, but this is the only current legal requirement for a complaints procedure at school level.)

The Commissioner should be consulted by ministers on the creation of new complaints procedures which would be used by children and young people (eg the prison ombudsperson and local education ombudspeople which some organisations have proposed).

(ii) Individual complaints

It would be unrealistic and in the current context unhelpful to children and young people and wasteful of resources to give the Commissioner the role of investigating individual complaints from the UK's 13.2 million children and young people under 18. To try to fulfil this role without large resources and a substantial network of local offices and advocacy schemes would mean offering children a remote and inaccessible centralised system. It is clear that children are unlikely to use procedures that are not local and readily accessible. It could also duplicate or conflict with the procedures and sources of help already available to children and young people, some of which are recent and very welcome developments. For example, IRCHIN (Independent Representation for Children in Need) and A Voice for the Child in Care have agreed to establish a national service to provide children in need with independent advice, advocacy and representation.

At a later stage it may be possible if the resources are available and in the light of the Commissioner's work so far to add to his/her role - or create separately - a carefully designed local or regional system to receive and investigate children's complaints across a defined range of services, together with a network of advocates to support children in making complaints. Such a system could benefit from the work the Commissioner had already done on improving existing complaints procedures. In the special case of the 80,000 or so children in care there may be a more urgent case for providing an independent body to receive complaints which are not satisfactorily resolved at a local level. Unlike other children in England and Wales, children in care will not have the right to seek to challenge their parenting by local authorities in court - others will have this right under section 8 of the Children Act 1989. And the Secretary of State's powers to intervene under section 84 of the Act are limited. This need could be met by establishing a new office or by providing the Commissioners for Local Administration with the resources and any necessary additional powers to fulfil the role.

In exceptional cases however the wide powers of the Commissioner to initiate investigations could enable him/her to investigate an individual case (the Commissioner's powers here would be as for other investigations). We would expect this to be limited to cases which raise important questions of principle which the Commissioner cannot tackle in other ways. Another possibility which could be examined is that the Commissioner should be able to refer particular cases to the Commissioners for Local Administration for investigation, when there is no other appropriate procedure, even where they currently fall outside the Local Commissioners' remit.

(iii) Referral and advice

The Commissioner's office would inevitably receive requests for advice, advocacy and information from children and young people and from adults acting on their behalf, although given the services already available it would not seek them. There are already a number of sources of help and advice for children and young people, and many local agencies. There is no point in the Commissioner duplicating advice services already provided in the voluntary sector, for example by the Children's Legal Centre and the Scottish Child Law Centre. Nor should the Commissioner seek to provide counselling, available through ChildLine and many local projects.

The Commissioner's office would have to respond to enquiries sensitively and effectively, although it will generally be most appropriate to refer requests to national or local organisations providing assistance to children or to particular complaints procedures.

The Commissioner's office should avoid merely giving a child or young person calling another phone number to ring. With the permission of the child or young person the Commissioner's staff should pass the complaint or request directly on to the relevant body, where appropriate asking to be informed in due course of the outcome. Otherwise the Commissioner would operate according to strict rules of confidentiality on any approaches from children and young people. Advice should not be given to an adult where this could conflict with the rights or interests of the child concerned.

D. The courts

The Commissioner would be able to assist with legal actions in exceptional cases, having powers to support and assist children or where necessary adults or organisations acting on their behalf in getting legal advice and taking legal action. The Commissioner's staff would include at least one solicitor with expertise in children's law - essential for detailed work on legislation and policy, but also enabling the office to act on occasion as a legal firm. (If the Commissioner requires specialist legal advice which was not available within the staff, it could be sought through his/her power to obtain professional advice of any kind - eg seeking counsel's opinion.)

Providing legal advice and assistance would not be a priority due to the existence of the Children's Legal Centre, the Scottish Child Law Centre and various local community law centres and firms of solicitors which specialise in law affecting children and young people. However the Commissioner would be able to assist with legal action on important questions of principle when in the Commissioner's opinion it was the necessary way to pursue the issues involved.

The Commissioner should also have the power to initiate or participate in legal proceedings in his/her own name whenever s/he believes it is the best way to promote the interests of children and young people. This could obviate the need for litigation to be conducted by specific individuals, which may be particularly difficult or unwelcome for children and young people. This would be analogous to the power local authorities have to institute or participate in legal proceedings where they 'consider it expedient for the promotion or protection of the interests of the inhabitants of their area'[6]. Similarly the Commission for Racial Equality and the Equal Opportunities Commission can institute legal proceedings in their own name in certain circumstances including persistent discrimination and discriminatory advertising.

E. Other activities

(i) International co-operation

We would expect the Commissioner to exchange information and co-operate with the many bodies promoting children's rights in other countries and to co-ordinate with them on international lobbying for children's rights, especially within the European Community. The Commissioner would probably develop particular links with similar offices elsewhere (see appendix 2).

(ii) Official inquiries

The Commissioner may wish to give evidence to official national and local inquiries affecting children and young people (eg child abuse inquiries, planning inquiries).

(iii) Grants to self-advocacy groups

The Commissioner should also have a specific power to give grants to self-advocacy organisations of children and young people or events intended to promote self-advocacy (we see no need for the Commissioner to have other grant-giving powers or to alter the way in which voluntary organisations working with and for children generally receive government grants).

(iv) UN Convention reports

Finally, the Commissioner should have a specific duty to consider and comment (before submission) on the report which the government must make every five years to the United Nations Committee on the Rights of the Child on its implementation of the Convention[7]. (The Commissioner may also at other times wish to draw the attention of this Committee to situations or events in the UK.) The government would be required to have regard to the Commissioner's comments.

4. Structure and ways of working

A. Location

The Commissioner and his/her staff would have an office in London. Despite the extra costs involved it would have to be situated in London to promote the most effective links with government departments, Parliament, most children's and professional organisations, and other bodies. The Commissioner's work is required throughout the UK but further consultation is necessary on the best means of operation in Scotland and Northern Ireland - in view of their different laws and political structures - and Wales. There may be an argument for linked Commissioners based in Edinburgh, Belfast and Cardiff. Alternatively, given that the principles underlying the Commissioner's work - the UN Convention and the other international treaties - apply throughout the UK, and that much policy affecting Scotland, Wales and Northern Ireland is made in London, it may be more effective to have a single Commissioner with four offices. If so, further thought will have to be given to the precise division of responsibilities between them.

B. Reporting arrangements

The Commissioner would report to the relevant Cabinet minister on issues which come under that minister. This is essential to tie the Commissioner in to decision-making structures. However some of the Commissioner's reports would cover general government responsibilities crossing departments. These should probably go to the Secretary of State for the department which has lead responsibility for children's issues ie currently the Department of Health (which we understand will also be responsible for overseeing implementation of the UN Convention). If a Minister for Children of Cabinet rank were appointed, as has been suggested, then s/he would clearly be the appropriate minister for this.

The Commissioner's annual report would be presented to Parliament. As well as reporting on his/her own activities, the Commissioner could include in his/her annual report a general description of the current situation of children and young people in the UK and important developments affecting them in the past year. (This would in some ways constitute a UK version of the report UNICEF produces each year, *The State of the World's Children.)*

C. Select Committee

We would also like to see a Parliamentary Select Committee set up specifically relating to the Commissioner's activities. Through its ability to question ministers and civil servants it could follow up on ministerial and departmental implementation of the Commissioner's recommendations and it would help raise the Parliamentary profile of the Commissioner's work. It would also be a useful public forum for discussion of the Commissioner's activities. The relationships between the Parliamentary Commissioner for Administration and the linked Select Committee, and that between the National Audit Office and the Public Accounts Committee, seem to be successful examples of a connection between independent statutory offices and Select Committees. (The creation of Select Committees is a matter for Parliament rather than the government.)

We would expect the Commissioner to have a close informal relationship with the All Party Parliamentary Group for Children.

D. Public profile

We envisage that the Commissioner would wish to maintain a high public profile and work closely with the media in highlighting issues affecting children and young people which should be of public concern.

E. Input from children and young people

It is important that there is direct input from children and young people into the Commissioner's work. The Commissioner may have to consider a number of strategies to achieve this. For example, s/he could organise local or national forums of children and young people to discuss his/her work. S/he could also have advisory groups of children and young people which could discuss priorities for the Commissioner's work and the stance the Commissioner should adopt on various issues, or a network of regional advisory groups which would allow the involvement of more children and young people. Specialist advisory groups could be formed, eg of children in care, adopted children, children with disabilities etc. Any advisory groups or forums could either deal with the Commissioner's overall activities or be related to particular topics which the Commissioner was currently working on or contemplating doing so. The Commissioner would also have to consider how to keep in touch with the needs of categories of children who cannot be directly represented in these ways for reasons of say age or severe learning difficulties.

The Commissioner would also maintain close contact with national and local organisations of children and young people, and ones which involve children and young people or have them as members. S/he could also try to request feedback through publications which children and young people read or television or radio programmes which they watch or listen to, or the Commissioner's own materials aimed at children and young people. The Commissioner might also wish to conduct opinion research amongst children and young people on certain topics.

Input from children and young people into the Commissioner's work would of course also result from the letters and phone calls which the Commissioner would anyway receive from them, and from direct contact through other parts of the Commissioner's work eg investigations.

F. Liaison with outside organisations

The Commissioner would stress maintaining close links with voluntary bodies and professional associations as well as statutory agencies involved with children and young people. The Commissioner would clearly wish to keep in close touch with developments on the ground and to benefit from the knowledge and expertise of others. The Commissioner may wish to organise regular meetings, conferences or seminars with such groups, either on particular topics or generally to discuss his/her activities. S/he might wish to hold an annual discussion forum on his/her work. The Commissioner would need to maintain a close relationship throughout the year with particular voluntary bodies working for children and young people.

G. Staffing and funding

The Commissioner would be able to appoint his/her own staff. (As stated in section 2, we advocate a Commissioner with a team of staff rather than a Commission, because it would help promote a better public profile and be more efficient, flexible, decisive and dynamic.) The Commissioner will need staff with a commitment to the principles of the UN Convention. S/he will require staff with a specialist knowledge in law, policy and practice affecting children and young people who are responsible for particular policy areas, and s/he will also need staff with the following functions among others: investigations, legal matters, media and PR work, information, liaison with outside bodies, and finance and internal support and administration. The Commissioner would also be able to use and pay for specialist advice from outside consultants as necessary. S/he may want to take on outside specialists to assist with particular reports and investigations, given the range of issues and services covered.

The Commissioner's remit is wide, and careful prioritisation of work will be essential. The level of resources available to the Commissioner will be important, and the greater those resources the greater will be the number of issues within the many possible areas of concern that the Commissioner is able to tackle effectively. We envisage that a reasonable level of staff would be about 50 with an annual budget (at 1991 prices) of around £2 million[8].

The Commissioner's office could either be funded through a separate Vote (as applies to some public bodies, for example the Charity Commission, OFTEL, OFGAS and OFWAT) or through a departmental budget, which would be that of the Department of Health. The advantage of the former seems to be that it generally offers greater stability and more independence, whereas in the latter case a powerful and sympathetic Secretary of State may be able to win greater resources.

H. Method of appointment

The Commissioner would be formally appointed by the Queen on the recommendation of (for the reasons given above) the Secretary of State for Health. If a Select Committee is created then the appointment could also be subject to the approval of the Select Committee Chair, similar to the procedure for appointing the Comptroller and Auditor General, who is head of the National Audit Office[9]. To maximise the Commissioner's protection from political and particularly government pressure, s/he could only be removed following resolutions of both Houses of Parliament. Many other appointments to public offices where independence is required have a similar safeguard[10]. The Commissioner would be appointed for a renewable fixed term, probably five years. In making the appointment the personal attributes of candidates such as commitment to the principles of the UN Convention, a wide understanding of the circumstances of children and services provided for them, the ability to form and maintain effective relationships with ministers and other bodies, and the ability to communicate well through the media, will be more important than specific qualifications. The post should be advertised and subject to open competition.

Alternatively the appointment should be made after consultation with relevant organisations including voluntary bodies.

I. Title

'Children's Rights Commissioner' or 'Children's Commissioner' seem the most appropriate titles. We have discarded the most obvious alternative - 'Children's Ombudsperson' - because the chief focus of the post will be on influencing policy rather than investigating complaints.

5. Creating the Commissioner

Legislation will be required to establish the Commissioner to ensure the office is created on a stable basis and with the necessary legal powers. Section 4 lists points which legislation should cover.

6. Conclusion

Creating a Children's Rights Commissioner would be an important reform for the UK's 13.2 million children and young people. Its work would improve law, policy and practice affecting children and young people; raise the status of children and young people in policy-making; and ensure that politicians, policy-makers and practitioners take children's rights and interests more seriously. Policy affecting children would take more account of children's rights and interests and the need for co-ordination, and would be based on a better understanding of its impact on children and young people and their perspective. The Commissioner's work would also result in better systems for children who are victims of injustice to obtain redress, and in less ill-treatment. Finally it would help the UK fulfil its obligations under the UN Convention on the Rights of the Child.

What arguments are there against creating such a Commissioner? There are potential differences of view on detail (eg the scope of the Commissioner's role) which could be expressed by those who support the suggestion in principle, but fundamental objections could be made either on the ground that the proposal goes much too far, or on the ground that it does not go nearly far enough.

Some people concerned about children's rights may support the creation of a much more elaborate and powerful body, with an extensive network of local offices, able to instruct ministers, local authorities, voluntary organisations and others, to follow its decisions and policies both on general matters and individual cases. (This could even extend to a role of handling complaints from children about their parents on issues not sufficiently serious to involve the social services.) Indeed when proposing the creation of a new institution it is tempting to suggest that it should have as many resources and powers as possible. This would be a very different plan from our proposal and we have explained at various points above why we think it is better to be less ambitious.

Others may think that the proposal goes too far on the basis that it is not the responsibility of government to rectify the problems outlined in section 2 by setting up a public body with public money. There are at least 1500 independent public bodies in the UK spending varying and in some cases large sums of public money. In our view many of them are highly effective in achieving for the government benefits to the community which it would be more difficult or impossible to achieve otherwise, and they therefore represent good value for money. The benefits derived justify the public spending.

Creating a Children's Rights Commissioner as proposed is a practical and realistic proposal for effective and efficient government action to meet the needs we have described.

Notes

1. Section 1(2) (Note this only applies in England and Wales, as do most references given here to specific Acts)
2. See section 26, Local Government and Housing Act 1989
3. See section 23, Courts and Legal Services Act 1990
4. See appendix C in the *Annual Report of the Council on Tribunals for 1986/7*, HMSO, 1988
5. See for example E Grey, *Children in the UK: Signposts to Statistics*, National Children's Bureau, 1982, and Jonathan Bradshaw, *Child Poverty and Deprivation in the UK*, National Children's Bureau, 1990. Currently the most useful regular collection of statistics about children and young people in the UK is the *Children in Danger Factfile* produced each year by National Children's Home.
6. See section 222, Local Government Act 1972
7. This is required by Article 44 of the Convention. The first report must be within two years of the Convention's entry into force in the state concerned.
8. For comparison levels of staffing and expenditure for some other public bodies are as follows:

Audit Commission: 763 staff, £33.9 million
Broadcasting Standards Council: 14 staff, £1.1 million
Commission for Local Administration (England): 95 staff, £2.7 million
Commission for Racial Equality: 196 staff, £11.8 million
Council on Tribunals: 14 staff, £0.5 million
Equal Opportunities Commission: 143 staff, £3.9 million
National Audit Office*: 900 staff, £31.5 million
National Consumer Council: 58 staff, £2.1 million
National Curriculum Council: 96 staff, £7.3 million
National Youth Bureau: 50 staff, £1.3 million
Official Solicitor's Department*: 134 staff, £4.2 million
Police Complaints Authority: 55 staff, £2.2 million
Social Services Inspectorate (England)*: 210 staff, £5 million

(The figures are for 1989/90 except that an asterisk indicates they are for 1990/91. Most are taken from *Public Bodies 1990,* a listing of 1,539 QUANGOs published by HMSO; the others were obtained directly from the bodies concerned.)
9. See section 1(1), National Audit Act 1983
10. For example, the Parliamentary Commissioner for Administration - see section 1(3), Parliamentary Commissioner Act 1967

Framework for Legislation - The Children's Rights Commissioner Act

Section 4

This section sets out the more important points that the statute setting up the Commissioner would have to cover, providing an indication of the nature of the legislation which we anticipate would be required. It is not intended to be a draft Bill, which would be more precise and complex. For the sake of convenience, legislative language is used (although while statutes currently use only male pronouns when referring to people of either gender, we have used 'he or she', etc).

Legislation should cover the following points (in a more detailed and rigorous manner and with appropriate qualifications). Points in square brackets are optional.

Appointment etc

1. For the purpose of promoting the rights of children, there shall be a Children's Rights Commissioner.

2. The Commissioner shall be appointed by Her Majesty on the recommendation of the Secretary of State for Health.

[3. Before making a recommendation the Secretary of State shall consult with such persons as appear to him or her to be appropriate.]

4. The Commissioner shall be appointed for a period of five years, and shall hold office during this period unless relieved at his or her own request or removed by Her Majesty in consequence of addresses from both Houses of Parliament.

5. At the end of a term of appointment the Commissioner shall be eligible for re-appointment.

6. The Commissioner may appoint such staff as he or she thinks fit to assist with the discharge of the Commissioner's functions.

7. Any function of the Commissioner may be performed by any member of the Commissioner's staff authorised for that purpose by the Commissioner.

8. The Commissioner and the Commissioner's staff shall not be regarded as agents or servants of the Crown.

Duties

9. The Commissioner shall have the following duties:

(a) to promote the rights and interests of children;

(b) to seek to ensure that the rights and interests of children are properly taken into account by Ministers of the Crown, government departments, local authorities, other public bodies and voluntary and private organisations when decisions on policies affecting children are taken;

(c) to promote compliance with the United Nations Convention on the Rights of the Child as set out in Schedule A, and such other international treaties, conventions or agreements (subject to any reservations made) which have been ratified or otherwise acceded to by Her Majesty's Government and which affect children, including those listed in Schedule B; and

(d) to seek to ensure that children have effective means of redress if their rights are disregarded by any body mentioned in (b) above.

10. The Secretary of State for Health may by order made by statutory instrument amend Schedule A (in respect of reservations made to the Convention) and Schedule B.

11. A draft of any report which it is intended shall be submitted by Her Majesty's Government to the Committee on the Rights of the Child under Article 44 of the United Nations Convention on the Rights of the Child shall be sent to the Commissioner, who shall consider it and respond, and Her Majesty's Government shall have regard to the Commissioner's response in finalising the report.

12. The Commissioner shall from time to time, when he or she thinks fit or is so required by the Secretary of State for Health, review the working of this Act and submit to the Secretary of State proposals for amending it.

13. In exercising his or her functions the Commissioner shall have regard to:

(a) the principles laid down in the United Nations Convention on the Rights of the Child as set out in Schedule A, and such other international treaties, conventions or agreements (subject to any reservations made) which have been ratified or otherwise acceded to by Her Majesty's Government and which affect children, including those listed in Schedule B;

(b) the need to ensure co-ordination between different bodies (including government departments) which provide services for children; and

(c) the need to consult from time to time with children and other persons seeking to promote the interests of children.

Reports and recommendations

14. The Commissioner shall submit an annual report on his or her activities to the Secretary of State for Health, who shall lay it before both Houses of Parliament and cause it to be published.

15. An annual report may also contain a general description of the circumstances of children in the United Kingdom and a survey of developments which have affected them during the period to which it relates.
16. The Commissioner may make other reports at his or her discretion, and may publish them as he or she thinks fit, and the reports may contain such recommendations for action by others (including Ministers of the Crown) which the Commissioner feels are necessary or expedient.
17. The Commissioner shall give his or her reasons for any recommendations in a report and shall send a copy of the report to any person to whom a recommendation is directed.
18. Any person to whom a recommendation is directed shall:
(a) consider that recommendation and have regard to it in determining what course of action to take as a result; and
(b) notify the Commissioner within three months of the report being sent (or a longer period if the Commissioner agrees) of the action which has been taken or it is intended to take in response to the recommendation.
19. If any person to whom a recommendation is directed intends not to comply with it then he or she shall furnish the Commissioner with his or her reasons for not doing so, and the Commissioner may publicise these reasons.
20. The Commissioner may require a person at whom a recommendation has been directed to furnish the Commissioner with such information as may be reasonably required to verify whether the recommendation has been complied with.
21. If it appears to the Commissioner that a particular body is not complying with the stipulations of the UN Convention, then the Commissioner may issue a recommendation in the form of a compliance notice, which shall state the Commissioner's opinion as to the way in which the Convention is not being complied with and what action should be taken to comply.
22. Points (18), (19) and (20) apply to compliance notices in the same way that they apply to other recommendations.
23. Any person who fails to comply (whether wholly or partly) with a compliance notice shall publicise that failure in such manner as the Commissioner may specify.
24. If the Commissioner has reasonable cause for believing that the person will not comply with point (23) above then he or she may publicise the failure to comply with the notice and recover any reasonable expenses incurred from the person whose failure has been publicised.
25. The Commissioner shall establish and maintain a register of compliance notices, and this register may be inspected at all reasonable hours by any person.
26. The Commissioner may from time to time publish and disseminate such guidance about good practice as he or she thinks fit in the furtherance of his or her duties.

Investigations

27. The Commissioner may conduct a formal investigation for any purpose connected with the carrying out of his or her duties.

28. For the purposes of a formal investigation the Commissioner may require any person who possesses documents or information relevant to the investigation to:

(a) produce such documents; and/or

(b) furnish the information in writing; and/or

(c) attend at a specified time and place and give oral information.

29. No person shall be compelled under point (28) to give information or produce documents which he or she could not be compelled to give or produce in civil proceedings before the High Court.

30. The Commissioner shall prepare and publish a report of his or her findings in any formal investigation and shall include in it such recommendations as appear to him or her to be necessary or expedient.

Relationship with Ministers and government departments

31. If a Minister of the Crown proposes to lay before Parliament a Bill which consists of or contains an amendment to or repeal of the whole or part of any enactment listed in Schedule C, he or she shall first consult the Commissioner.

32. If a Minister of the Crown proposes to consider a Bill laid before Parliament other than by him or her which consists of or contains an amendment to or repeal of the whole or part of any enactment listed in Schedule C, he or she shall first consult the Commissioner.

33. If a Minister of the Crown proposes to make an order under any section of an enactment where that section is mentioned in the list in Schedule D, he or she shall first consult the Commissioner.

34. When consulted under points (31), (32) or (33) the Commissioner shall consider and respond to the Minister's proposals, and the Minister shall have regard to the Commissioner's response.

35. The Secretary of State for Health may by order made by statutory instrument add to (but not subtract from) the list of enactments in Schedule C and of sections of enactments in Schedule D.

36. There shall be a code of consultation relating to the consultation of the Commissioner by government departments.

37. The code shall be determined by agreement between the Commissioner and the Secretary of State for Health.

38. Government departments shall have regard to the code of consultation.

[OR

36. For each government department there shall be a code of consultation relating to the consultation of the Commissioner by that department.

37. For each department the code shall be determined by agreement between the Commissioner and a Minister in that department.
38. Each department shall have regard to the code of consultation relating to it.]

39. Whenever it appears necessary or expedient to the Commissioner, he or she may require a Minister of the Crown to provide a child impact statement relating to any decision or proposal on policy which affects children which the Minister has made.
40. Any child impact statement so required shall set out the probable impact in the Minister's opinion on children of the decision or proposal to which the statement relates, and the Minister shall cause the statement to be published.
41. Where the Commissioner publishes his or her opinions with regard to a child impact statement and requests the Minister who provided the statement to respond to these opinions, the Minister shall do so.
42. Where a Minister requests the Commissioner to consider or report on a particular matter other than under points (31), (32) or (33) above, the Commissioner shall have regard to that request.

Complaints procedures

43. The Commissioner may require any person who has a statutory duty to establish, operate or supervise any procedure for the consideration of representations or complaints to provide such information as can reasonably be obtained about the number, nature and outcomes of representations or complaints made by or on behalf of children.
44. The Commissioner may request such information from any person who has established, operates or supervises any other procedure for the consideration of representations or complaints.
45. Information provided to the Commissioner under points (43) or (44) shall not identify any person who has made a representation or complaint.
46. The guidance about good practice which the Commissioner may publish and disseminate under point (26) above may include a code of good practice for procedures for the consideration of representations or complaints.

Other powers and functions

47. The Commissioner may publish and disseminate such information about children which appears to him or her to be necessary or expedient for the carrying out of his or her duties.
48. The Commissioner may undertake or assist (financially or otherwise) the undertaking by other persons of any research which appears to him or her to be necessary or expedient for the carrying out of his or her duties.
49. Where the Commissioner considers it necessary or expedient for the promotion or protection of the interests or rights of children, he or she may:

(a) prosecute or defend or appear in any legal proceedings and, in the case of civil proceedings, institute them in his or her own name; and

(b) in his or her own name make representations in the interests of children at any public inquiry held by or on behalf of any Minister or public body under any enactment.

50. Where the Commissioner considers it necessary or expedient for the carrying out of his or her duties, the Commissioner may give assistance to a child or to a person acting on behalf of a child.

51. The assistance the Commissioner may give may include giving advice (including legal advice) or arranging for legal advice or for legal representation.

52. In deciding whether to give such assistance the Commissioner shall have regard to:

(a) the availability of such assistance elsewhere;

(b) whether in the Commissioner's opinion an important question of principle is involved; and

(c) what is in the Commissioner's opinion the most efficient and effective means for the discharge of his or her duties.

53. The Commissioner may give financial or other assistance to any organisation for the purpose of encouraging the promotion by children of the interests of children.

Schedules

Schedule A: the text of the United Nations Convention on the Rights of the Child, taking into account reservations made by Her Majesty's Government.

Schedule B: a list of other international treaties, conventions or agreements which Her Majesty's Government has ratified or otherwise acceded to and which affect children.

Schedule C: a list of enactments which Ministers shall not be able to amend or repeal without having first consulted the Commissioner.

Schedule D: a list of sections of enactments under which Ministers shall not be able to make orders without having first consulted the Commissioner.

Appendix 1

Recent Proposals to Increase Representation of Children's Rights and Interests

Various proposals have been made in the last two decades aimed at improving representation of children's and young people's interests at central government level. The variety of ideas indicates wide recognition of the need. One of the first was from Brian Jackson, then Director of the National Education Development Trust, who, writing in 1976 in *New Society*[1], proposed a Minister for Children: 'Even the most junior Minister for Children could exert a colossal effect by raising the child question, publicly, at the right political moment'. Other commentators were sceptical: 'The post would most likely be at a junior minister level comparable, say, with the Minister for the Disabled - no money, no power, no real influence, a prey to official pressure. In short, it would end up as a public relations post, excusing government policy rather than making it', wrote Rick Rogers in *The Guardian*[2].

The only governmental or statutory initiative to get off the ground in the UK has been the Children's Committee. This stemmed from the Committee on Child Health Services, the Court Committee, which published its report, *Fit for the Future*[3], in 1976. The report proposed the formation of a Children's Committee as a joint committee of the Central Health Services Council and the Personal Social Services Council, two existing governmental advisory bodies.

The recommendation was accepted, and the Children's Committee was established in 1978 by the Secretaries of State for Health and Social Security and Wales and in consultation with the Secretary of State for Education and Science. Its terms of reference were: 'To advise the Secretaries of State on the co-ordination and development of health and personal social services as they relate to children and families with children'. Its members were appointed as individuals with relevant expertise; it had independent status, a small secretariat, and was funded by the Department of Health and Social Security.

The Children's Committee had a brief but active life, forming working groups and producing publications on *The Reduction of Perinatal Mortality and Morbidity* (June 1979), *Services for Adolescents* (April 1980), *Out of Hours Social and Health Care* (June 1980), *The Needs of Under-Fives in the Family* (January 1981), *The Representation of Children's Rights and Interests* (September 1981), and *Corporal Punishment* (October 1981), as well as providing advice on other issues, and organising conferences.

In 1981 the Secretary of State for Social Services announced that given the new Government's policy to retain only those non-departmental public bodies which were 'clearly essential', the Secretary of State 'did not consider that the Children's Committee passed this test'[4]. In a statement responding to its closure, the members of the Committee wrote: '... The members believe that their attempt to consider the needs of children across the boundaries of professions, services and traditions has enabled them to argue for the interests of children in the formulation of policy and in the implementation of practice. To this extent they fear a gap will be left as a result of the Committee's closure'[5]. In their personal capacity the members resolved 'to explore with urgency the possibility of creating a framework for a Children's Council so that all who are persuaded of the need for a voice for children may secure an independent means of working collaboratively to influence Parliament and to improve public understanding of the needs of children'.

In its own report on *The Representation of Children's Rights and Interests*, the Committee discussed other proposed initiatives including a Minister for Children, an Inter-Departmental Advisory Council, a Children's Ombudsperson and a Children's Commission or Council 'standing apart from government but relating closely to it'. It also welcomed the formation of the Children's Legal Centre, which had just been set up following International Year of the Child (1979).

Commenting on the ombudsperson proposal, the report indicates that supporters of the idea did not wish to limit the scope of the office to dealing with individual cases: 'The handling of specific cases would, it is claimed, help to codify the rights of children and indicate new legislation necessary to remedy ambiguities in the protection the law extends to children'. The children's ombudsperson 'would also enter the arena of policy debate by generally drawing attention to the needs of children and speaking for their interests to Royal Commissions and Committees of Enquiry'. The report indicated that there had been attempts to amend the Children Act 1975 during its parliamentary passage to create such an office, 'but this effort to create a framework which would actively promote children's interests in the broadest sense was not successful'.

The report concluded by seeking responses to the Children's Committee's assessment of the need for an independent Children's Council 'which, extending across the boundaries of professional and agency interests, can press for the shaping and development of policies and legislation which effectively meet the needs of children and their families'.

Following the death of the Children's Committee, some of those involved obtained funding from the Calouste Gulbenkian Foundation and the Buttle Trust for a further inquiry. Chaired by Professor Nicholas Deakin (a member of the Advisory Group for the current study), its terms of reference were to consult with relevant statutory, voluntary and professional bodies and other interested groups 'to determine whether there is a case for an independent national grouping concerned with the advocacy of children's interests'. It was to go on to identify the 'principles and purpose to be adopted by any such grouping', and to make proposals for constitution and funding.

The overwhelming response to the consultation stage of the inquiry was that there was a 'strong argument' for creating such a body, so the inquiry went on to the second stage - 'consideration of the ways in which the gap which evidently existed could be filled'. The report of the inquiry, *A Voice for All Children*[6], published in 1982, considered deficiencies in society's treatment of children and possible reasons for them, the experience of the Children's Committee, and options for a new organisation. Among the options considered but not pursued were a Minister for Children, a permanent Cabinet Committee with responsibility for policy on children, an organisation linked to a House of Commons select committee, and a Children's Ombudsperson.

The report concluded by proposing two options. The first was an independent Children's Council, a small body of independent experts with a small permanent secretariat and access to research facilities 'to address major policy issues across the whole age range in an authoritative way'. The second option was a Children's Congress and Children's Trust: a national conference or 'congress' of representatives of all agencies that have an interest in the welfare of children would elect a steering committee to provide continuity between congresses. It in turn would appoint a small group of permanent trustees. The final conclusion of the report was that the initial approach should be to create a small independent Children's Council, but that an item for early exploration would be moving towards a broader framework with a congress and trust.

In the event, various initiatives in the voluntary sector followed publication of *A Voice for All Children*. The National Children's Bureau appointed a multi-disciplinary group which came to be called the Child Policy Review Group, and the Children's Legal Centre organised two congresses, in 1984 and again in 1986, on 'Children and their Rights'. The congress held in November 1984 brought together 250 representatives from more than 100 organisations working with or for children and young people. It coincided with the 25th anniversary of the adoption of the UN Declaration of the Rights of the Child, and it was addressed in a plenary session by Målfrid Grude Flekkøy[7], the Norwegian Children's Ombudsperson.

Public discussion of related ideas has continued. In Parliament there were attempts to raise the idea of a children's ombudsperson during the passage of the Children Act 1989, and also of education ombudspeople, to whom school students would have access, during the passage of the Education Reform Act 1988.

Most recently, late in 1990, the Review of Child Care Law in Scotland[8] was published, proposing amongst over 90 detailed recommendations that the Secretary of State for Scotland should commission an examination of the case for and feasibility of a Child Welfare Commission in Scotland.

As noted in section 1, in their discussion of the idea the Review Group suggest an office some of whose functions are similar to those of the proposed Children's Rights Commissioner: 'The case for a Child Welfare Commission cannot be argued exclusively from the point of view of child care. It should be concerned with the whole range of public services which impact on the lives of children - care, education and health in particular. This points to the establishment of a Commission with the following principal functions: to monitor the effectiveness of the inspection and registration of residential child care establishments; to review and advise upon the provision of effective integrated health, education and welfare services for children; to undertake such inquires into public provisions for children as the Secretary of State or local authorities may commission; to advise children on their legal rights, on agency complaints and appeals procedures, and on how to initiate judicial reviews or appeals; to recommend changes in public policies relating to the interests and welfare of children'. The report proposes that appropriate powers of access to people and information would be needed. 'In addition, the Commission's coverage might mirror that of the UN Convention of the Rights of the Child, and indeed it has been suggested that it would play a key part in monitoring implementation of the Convention in Scotland.'

The Group's suggestion has received virtually unanimous backing from respondents to the Secretary of State for Scotland's request for comments. The Secretary of State is currently considering the results of consultation on the report's recommendations.

Notes

1. Brian Jackson, A Minister for Children?, *New Society*, 15 January, 1976
2. Rick Rogers, Giving Children a Voice of their Own, *The Guardian*, 2 October, 1979
3. *Fit for the Future*, Report of the Committee on Child Health Services, HMSO, 1976
4. Department of Health and Social Security press release, 11 June, 1981
5. Closure of the Children's Committee: statement from members, 22 June, 1981
6. *A Voice for all Children*, Report of an Independent Committee of Inquiry, Bedford Square Press/NCVO, 1982
7. *Agenda for Children* - a Report on Congress 84: Children and their Rights, Children's Legal Centre, 1985
8. *Review of Child Care Law in Scotland*, Report of a Review Group appointed by the Secretary of State, HMSO, 1990

International Developments

Children's rights are now an important concern internationally. The International Year of the Child in 1979 helped to make the issues more prominent, leading in many countries to significant developments in the 1980s. And the adoption of the United Nations Convention in 1989 has focused attention on children's rights and how they can be protected virtually throughout the world.

Since Norway established the post of *Barneombud* (Children's Ombudsperson) in 1981, there has been an international trend towards (a) recognising the lack of input from a children's perspective into many decisions which affect them; and (b) consequently the creation of institutions to promote children's interests and rights (at national or local levels) with the following important characteristics: (i) the institution is established by a public authority and has some sort of official status; (ii) it is substantially if not completely independent in actions and attitudes; (iii) it has a wide-ranging remit across different policy areas.

In other respects the institutions created naturally take different forms in the light of different constitutions, political traditions and the specific circumstances of children and young people. The most important developments from the point of view of this report are those in Norway, New Zealand and Australia. These are described below, along with developments at the European-wide level and a brief summary of various measures which have been taken in some other countries[1].

Norway

An Act establishing the post of *Barneombud* (Children's Ombudsperson) was passed by the Norwegian Parliament in March 1981 and the first postholder, Målfrid Grude Flekkøy, took office in September 1981. In 1989 after two four-year terms (the maximum allowed) she was succeeded by Trond-Viggo Torgersen.

The idea had been discussed for several years before 1981. It was recommended in 1977 by a committee established by the Ministry of Justice and was examined in 1979 by an inter-departmental committee of the six ministries with responsibilities for children. This was followed by the Bill in the 1980-81 session of Parliament.

The *Barneombud* is autonomous and has the statutory duty to 'promote the interests of children vis-à-vis public and private authorities'. The office works by recommending legal or policy changes to central and local government and politicians; using the media; distributing information on children's rights; investigating and taking up individual cases; and raising issues of principle which arise from them. It has no power to take decisions itself or revoke or alter decisions taken by the authorities. In carrying out investigations it has a statutory right of access to children's institutions and otherwise confidential information and records. The only cases it cannot investigate are conflicts between children and their parents, and cases which have been taken to court.

The *Barneombud* is consulted formally by government as part of the consultative 'hearings' process which Norwegian ministries conduct before legislative proposals are presented to Parliament. This enables the *Barneombud* to comment on them from a children's perspective and in eight years Mrs Flekkøy responded to about 150 proposals covering all policy areas.

The issues which have featured most prominently in the *Barneombud's* work can be divided into the following six areas[2]:

(i) children in special circumstances - including child abuse, child protection, and children living in institutions such as hospitals and prisons;

(ii) child care and leisure facilities - kindergartens and day nurseries, other kinds of pre-school care, youth clubs etc;

(iii) schooling - use of school buildings, poor school transport, difficulties encountered by disabled children, exclusion procedures etc;

(iv) cultural and consumer problems - including dangerous products, accident prevention at home, and children's television;

(v) family circumstances - problems for children stemming from family financial, employment or housing circumstances, etc;

(vi) urban and rural planning - planning of roads, housing developments, local facilities etc.

Initially Mrs Flekkøy concentrated on investigating and assisting with individual cases but later she gave increased priority to pursuing issues of principle and policy change. Specific changes which the *Barneombud* has helped to achieve since 1981 include the following:

● new regulations concerning the rights of hospitalised children, giving the child the right to have parents with him/her at all times and the right to pre-school, ordinary school or special education while in hospital;

● raising the age at which young people can be imprisoned in adult prisons;

● legislation prohibiting all forms of physical punishment of children;

● a requirement that all local Building Boards (which regulate local planning) have a special official responsible for monitoring plans for their impact on children;

● legislative recognition of the right of children to know both their parents, regardless of their marital status;

● tighter building regulations on safe housing and accident prevention in the home.

The *Barneombud* is now well-established in Norway as a popular and respected institution. An opinion poll in 1989 showed that 83% of Norwegians thought it should continue, with 15% don't knows and only 2% in favour of abolishing it. Although its creation was controversial and only passed through Parliament by five votes, it now has strong support across the political spectrum. This Norwegian initiative has also aroused a great deal of international interest.

New Zealand

In New Zealand the post of Commissioner for Children is more recent and is still at an early stage. It was created by the Children, Young Persons and Their Families Act 1989, and the first Commissioner, Dr Ian Hassall, took office in July 1989 for a five year term.

The idea of creating an advocate for children linked to the process of government was suggested during International Year of the Child, 1979. It aroused considerable interest and gained support from a number of bodies. Different possible schemes were discussed during a lengthy review of child protection legislation in the 1980s, and the Commissioner was incorporated into the Act which followed that review. The eventual model adopted for the Commissioner was strongly influenced by the Norwegian set-up and by the South Australian Children's Interests Bureau.

The Commissioner's functions as laid down in law fall into two broad areas:

The first is concerned with generally promoting the welfare of children and young people. In relation to this the Commissioner's functions are to undertake and promote research; to inquire into and report on any matter, including any enactment, law, practice or procedure; to receive representations from members of the public; to increase public awareness; and to encourage the development within the Department of Social Welfare of policies and services designed to promote the welfare of children and young people.

The second relates to overseeing the Children, Young Persons and Their Families Act 1989, which as well as creating the Commissioner is also the major piece of legislation on child protection. In this area the Commissioner's functions are to investigate decisions made or actions taken under the Act; to monitor and assess the policies and practices of the Department of Social Welfare and any other person or organisation performing functions under the Act; to advise Ministers on the administration of the Act; and to keep under review and make recommendations on the working of the Act.

The Commissioner acts independently, is appointed on the recommendation of the Minister for Social Welfare, and the funding for the Commissioner's staff and activities is approved by Parliament.

Since 1989 the Commissioner's main activities have included reviewing legislation, procedures and practice; representing children's interests through the media, in some court cases, and to legislators and government departments; investigating complaints; and promoting research and the establishment of an information base on children and their families.

In a paper prepared for a UNICEF seminar[3] in November 1990, Dr Hassall stated: 'In general terms what our office can do best is to influence policy, law and practice at central government level'. He added that he prefers independence and freedom of action to the possibility of being able to give directions to the Department of Social Welfare. He also emphasised the following other important principles for his activities: a reliable information base, community contacts, and commitment to the child's viewpoint.

Australia

Australia has a federal constitution under which each state has considerable autonomy. Developments at the state level are therefore important. The state of South Australia, which has a tradition of social reform, has set up an official Children's Interests Bureau.

The Bureau was established following amendments passed in 1983 to the Community Welfare Act, and it opened in 1984. The idea came originally from a survey of consumers' views on the (South Australia) Department for Community Welfare's services and received support in the aftermath of International Year of the Child.

The main functions originally laid down for the Bureau are to increase public awareness of the rights and welfare of children; to conduct research or inquiries into matters affecting the welfare of children; and to monitor and evaluate the policies of the Department for Family and Community Services (as the Department for Community Welfare is now called) in relation to children.

Further powers were added in 1988: to provide independent advice to the Department on the rights and interests of any child subject to proceedings dealing with his/her care and protection (especially before a court declares that the child is in need of care); and to participate in reviews of children under state guardianship. A Child Advocacy Unit was created within the Bureau to fulfil these functions. (The Bureau is currently being given a new statutory basis under a separate Act.)

The Bureau is partly independent and partly subject to the direction of the Minister for Family and Community Services who also appoints members of its advisory committee. Bureau staff are public servants and it is funded through the Department, but it is an entirely separate entity.

The Bureau's main activities include reviewing and making recommendations on law and policy affecting children; producing discussion papers; independent advocacy for children at case conferences and reviews; producing and distributing information and publications; representing children's interests to other bodies and the media; and giving advice.

The Bureau covers the full range of issues affecting children and their rights and welfare, including health, education, environment, family law and child protection. Specific issues it has taken up include the problems of child witnesses in court, corporal punishment, pupil participation in schools, children with AIDS, children and the hospital environment, the planning system and facilities for children on housing estates, custody and access disputes, adoption policies, the rights of children in care, reproductive technology and children's rights, and children's employment.

The creation of the Bureau received cross-party political support, and it has had a very productive relationship with the Minister for Family and Community Services (and opposition politicians) which has contributed to its success.

Europe

The Council of Europe is currently considering measures to promote children's rights in its member states. In February 1990 the Parliamentary Assembly (which consists of MPs nominated from the parliaments of member states) passed a resolution[4] calling on the Committee of Ministers (representatives of the governments) to examine the possibility of a Council of Europe legal instrument on children's rights to complement the UN Convention. This is now being looked at by the Council's inter-governmental Committee of Experts on Family Law, and it seems likely that a European treaty on children's rights will be drawn up.

This could take the form of an additional protocol to the European Convention on Human Rights, possibly containing some of the UN Convention's principles - eg the obligation to take account of children's views on matters affecting them and the requirement that the best interests of the child shall be a primary consideration in decision-making.

It seems probable that a European treaty would also focus on ensuring the existence of adequate mechanisms for promoting and enforcing the rights of children. This might involve a European-wide supra-national body or national bodies which might have the same sort of aims as the Children's Rights Commissioner. These developments could have a major impact throughout Europe, although the need for agreement between the member states means that it will be some time before decisions are reached.

Other Countries

Other countries where some similar steps have been taken include:

Canada: Canada is a federal nation and a number of individual states have created posts to defend children's rights. British Columbia has established a Deputy Ombudsman for Children and Youth within the state Ombudsman service to investigate complaints from children and young people and recommend policy changes. In Québec the *Comité de la protection de la jeunesse* protects the rights of minors who are subject to state legislation either on child protection or young offending through conducting investigations, making recommendations, taking legal action and initiating research. Alberta has a Children's Advocate who provides advocacy for children receiving services under the state Child Welfare Act, which covers child protection, and also advises the relevant Minister. In Ontario a similar role is played by the Office of Child and Family Service Advocacy.

Germany: An official Parliamentary Commission on Children's Affairs started work in 1988, consisting of one Bundestag member from each of the four main political parties. The Commission sees its main task as reviewing and influencing federal laws affecting children, and it seeks to promote the interests of children within the Bundestag (Parliament).

Austria: The Youth Welfare Act 1989 contained a broadly-worded provision under which Austria's provinces are to appoint 'children and youth advocates' to advise children, parents and legal representatives on all matters concerning the position of children and their upbringing and to assist with disputes.

Belgium: In French-speaking Belgium the local government is intending to appoint a *Délégué général aux droits de l'enfant et à l'aide à la jeunesse*, a post which will be based on although not identical to the Norwegian model.

Israel: In 1986 Jerusalem Council appointed a Children's Ombudsperson who investigates and seeks to resolve complaints from children. The Ombudsperson has also dealt with complaints from the rest of Israel.

Costa Rica: One country which has deliberately emulated the Norwegian Children's Ombudsperson is Costa Rica which in 1988 appointed a 'defender of children', *El Defensor de la Infancia*. The post is partly funded by UNICEF. The Defensor promotes research and campaigns about aspects of childhood, investigates children's complaints, and reviews legislation and institutional procedures which affect children.

Notes

1. Further information on a number of countries can be found in Eugeen Verhellen & Frans Spiesschaert (eds), *Ombudswork for Children*, published by Ghent University, Belgium. This is a collection of papers given at a conference held in December 1987.
2. For further information see Målfrid Grude Flekkøy, *A Voice for Children*, Jessica Kingsley Publishers, 1991.
3. International seminar on 'Models for monitoring the protection of children's rights', held in November 1990 at the UNICEF International Child Development Centre, Florence.
4. Recommendation 1121 (1990)

The Rights of Children and Young People to Make Complaints

Appendix 3

Children and young people use a wide variety of statutory services - education, health, social services etc - and others run by voluntary and private bodies. More than 200,000 children in the UK spend significant periods of their lives in a variety of institutions away from their 'natural' home: boarding schools, children's homes, secure units, hospitals, young offender institutions etc.

Over the last few years there has been an increasing recognition of the need for children to have ready access to well-publicised complaints procedures with an independent element (cases of serious abuse of children in both boarding schools and children's homes have provided the main impetus for reform). There are also now various voluntary sector advocacy schemes for children, and the proposed IRCHIN/A Voice for the Child in Care national service.

While preparing this report we sent a questionnaire to a wide range of statutory and non-statutory bodies which operate complaints procedures. We received replies from 30 bodies (see list at end of appendix). In general, whether complaints procedures relate to a particular service, eg the health service, or consumer complaints about gas or water supplies, or to particular issues, eg to those within the scope of the Equal Opportunities Commission and Commission for Racial Equality, children have the same access to them as adults.

The survey found that very few complaints are received from children (in the case of some procedures, no complaints had been received from under-18s since they were initiated). In some cases this is because the relevant services are available to very few children and young people. But in many cases it is clear that little attempt has been made to inform children and young people about the procedures, to make them readily accessible, or to reassure children and young people about the consequences of making complaints.

Central and Local Government Procedures etc

Social services

Section 26 of the Children Act 1989 provides (for England and Wales) the first statutory obligation to have a complaints procedure specifically aimed at children. By October 1991 local authority social services departments must have established procedures for considering 'any representations including complaints' made by children they are looking after, or other children who are within the Act's definition 'in need' (and also by parents, foster-parents and others). Complaints must be about the local authority's duties to support children and families - Part III of the Act. A similar obligation is placed on voluntary organisations and proprietors of registered (private) children's homes, in relation to children they are looking after.

Detailed draft guidance and regulations were issued by the Department of Health in September 1990. They envisage a two-stage process for local authority procedures: if the complaint is eligible it goes in the first stage to an independent person; if the complainant is not satisfied by the resolution of the complaint at this stage, it goes to a panel involving at least one (different) independent person.

The Children Act also gives the Secretary of State the power (under section 84) to intervene if satisfied that a local authority has failed to comply with any duty under the Act 'without reasonable excuse'. Such action could be initiated by representations from a child or group of children.

Several local authorities have set up complaints procedures with an independent element in advance of implementation of the Children Act; some have asked voluntary child welfare organisations to provide a service for them. Leicestershire has appointed a 'Children's Rights Officer' with a wider brief (and in Scotland Tayside has followed suit).

Also within the child care system there is an obligation on proprietors of residential care homes (generally for elderly people but including some children with disabilities and learning difficulties) to provide a complaints procedure for all residents. The Department of Health has introduced formal complaints procedures at both the Youth Treatment Centres which it administers; complaints may be made by residents about any aspect of their life in the YTC.

In Northern Ireland, Health and Social Services Boards are in the process of setting up complaints procedures for children and young people in children's homes (including voluntary homes).

Complaints about maladministration in personal social services may be made to the Commissioners for Local Administration (see below).

Health and mental health services

There are detailed procedures to enable patients including children to complain about hospital care, including clinical judgment, and about health care in the community. The National Health Service (Service Committees and Tribunals) Regulations 1974 as amended, issued under the National Health Service Act 1977, provide for formal investigation of complaints made by or on behalf of anyone entitled to family health services, alleging that a family practitioner has failed to comply with relevant terms of service.

Directions issued to health authorities under section 17 of the National Health Service Act 1977, following the Hospital Complaints Act 1985, provide a formal framework for complaints about hospital services, care or treatment. (Community Health Councils are empowered to assist patients to make complaints about health care.) There are similar provisions for Scotland in the National Health Service (Scotland) Act 1978. In Northern Ireland there are non-statutory complaints procedures relating to health services.

Complaints by patients detained or formerly detained under the Mental Health Act must be investigated by the Mental Health Act Commission (in Scotland and Northern Ireland there are separate Commissions).

Complaints can also be made to the Health Service Commissioner (see below) with regard to certain failures in services or maladministration by health authorities, family health service authorities, the Mental Health Act Commission and the Public Health Laboratory Service Board. In private health institutions (which must register as nursing homes or mental nursing homes) there is no obligation to have any internal complaints procedure. There are a number of children, including children with severe learning difficulties, in these institutions.

Education

Local education authorities in England and Wales are obliged to set up arrangements under section 23 of the Education Reform Act 1988 to consider complaints about specified actions of LEAs and governing bodies relating to the curriculum or religious worship in schools (similar arrangements apply to Education and Library Boards in Northern Ireland). Complaints may be made by anyone, including pupils (but the Department of Education and Science Circular 1/89, *Local Arrangements for the Consideration of Complaints*, makes no specific mention of pupil complainants at all). Grant-maintained schools are also obliged to set up a procedure for considering complaints about the curriculum (under section 58 of the Education Reform Act).

Complaints may be made to the Secretary of State for Education and Science under sections 68 and 99 of the Education Act 1944, as amended by section 219 of the Education Reform Act, about the conduct of LEAs and governing bodies of maintained schools, including grant-maintained schools, higher education corporations and certain institutions of further and higher education maintained or assisted by LEAs. If the complaints are about matters covered by the local procedure outlined above, they must have been considered by it first. Similarly, the Secretary of State for Scotland has the power to take default action following complaint under section 70 of the Education (Scotland) Act 1980.

Rights under education law to appeal to local appeal committees over such matters as school choice, special needs provision and school exclusion are exercisable only by parents and over-18s in England and Wales (also those aged 16 and over in Scotland).

The Children Act 1989 provides new protection for children in independent boarding schools in England and Wales: proprietors have a new duty to safeguard and promote the welfare of children, and social services have a duty to ensure that this happens. Detailed draft guidance has now been issued by the Department of Health which suggests that these schools should have a publicised and accessible complaints procedure, and also indicate to children how they can complain to someone independent of the school, and to the local authority social services department about any welfare matter. The Act also requires independent schools accommodating less than 50 pupils to register as children's homes; these schools will be obliged to set up a complaints procedure under the regulations to apply to children's homes.

Penal system

There are formal procedures for young people detained in young offender institutions and prisons to make complaints. There are a series of levels for complaint: to member of staff in charge of 'wing', application to governor, application to Board of Visitors, application to see Visiting Officer of the Secretary of State, petition to Secretary of State. The procedures are widely regarded as unsatisfactory, affected by a lack of confidentiality and fear of reprisals.

In Northern Ireland there are currently no formal complaints procedures for children and young people detained in the four training schools (there is a non-statutory system of independent volunteers visiting those detained in the one secure training school).

Social security

In general social security is not available below 16. Claims for social security are dealt with by independent adjudication officers; claimants who are unhappy with a decision can ask for a review or appeal to an independent tribunal. There is a further right of appeal on a point of law from the tribunal decision to the Social Security Commissioner and from the Commissioner's decision to an appropriate court. 16 and 17 year olds are not generally eligible for income support. Decisions on eligibility because 'severe hardship' will result if income support is not provided are made by the Severe Hardship Cases Unit in Glasgow, and may be reviewed following representation.

The Attendance Allowance Board determines medical questions arising from claims for Attendance Allowances; dissatisfied claimants can seek a review of the decision, and beyond that there is a right of appeal on a point of law to the Social Security Commissioner. Certain other matters, generally to do with contributions, are decided by the Secretary of State; claimants can seek a review on a point of law to an appropriate court.

Department of Trade and Industry

There are no formal procedures for considering complaints about matters falling within the Department's responsibilities. (The Office of Fair Trading was set up as an independent government department with no minister by the Fair Trading Act 1973; it has no powers to intervene in individual consumer complaints. Its purpose is to protect consumers by making sure that trading practices are as fair as possible and encouraging competition among businesses. It collects figures etc of complaints made to Trading Standards Departments, Environmental Health Departments, Consumer Advice Centres and Citizens' Advice Bureaux, all of which may receive complaints from under-18s.)

Employment

Any procedures that exist for complaints about employment are open to under-18s. A contractual requirement is placed on providers of youth training to ensure that non-employed trainees have access to clear written grievance procedures, including a right to make representations to the Department of Employment or local careers service. Training and Enterprise Councils must ensure that youth training providers make similar arrangements. There are no formal procedures for complaints about the careers service or the Department's Vocational Education Programmes (TVEI etc).

In Northern Ireland, under the Fair Employment (NI) Acts 1976 and 1989, complaints made by minors concerning unlawful discrimination on grounds of religious belief or political opinion must be brought by their parent or guardian.

Lord Chancellor's Department

The Lord Chancellor's Department says a formal but non-statutory procedure exists for considering any complaints made to the Lord Chancellor about matters falling within the responsibilities of the Department.

Other Channels for Complaints

Parliamentary Commissioner for Administration

The functions and responsibilities are set out in the Parliamentary Commissioner for Administration Act 1967 (as amended). No statistics are available on complaints received from or on behalf of under-18s. There is no restriction on the age of complainants, and no specific measures to encourage or discourage complaints from any particular group.

Health Service Commissioner

The Commissioner was established in 1973. The legislation is contained in the National Health Service Act 1977 as amended, and that for the Scottish Commissioner in the National Health Service (Scotland) Act 1978. The same person currently holds the offices of Parliamentary Commissioner and Health Service Commissioner, and the points made above under Parliamentary Commissioner also apply to the Health Service Commissioner.

Commission for Local Administration (local government ombudspeople)

Separate Commissions exist for England, Wales, Scotland and Northern Ireland. None has received many complaints from children. The Commissioners for Local Administration in England and Wales were appointed under the Local Government Act 1974, which has since been amended. They can investigate complaints of injustice arising from maladministration by local authorities and certain other local bodies. There are specific limits on the powers of investigation of the Commissioners which are relevant to children (eg no investigation of internal school matters; no initiation of an investigation without a specific complaint).

In England, in the year ended 31 March 1990, a total of 8,733 complaints were received by the three regional offices of the Commission. 302 of these were about education, of which 95% were from parents on behalf of children. Of 310 complaints about social services, about 20 came from children in care, most of them through the National Association of Young People in Care (NAYPIC). In one case the Commission issued a report about complaints of neglect and abuse in a London children's home. The investigation found 'considerable and serious maladministration' had caused injustice to three young women. The office covering the north of England has only received three complaints from under-18s in the last 15 years.

The Commission states that while parents can make complaints on behalf of children, 'if the child is of appropriate age and understanding, eg 14 plus, we would normally confirm with the child that he or she wished to have the complaint made on his or her behalf'. There is no requirement to seek consent from a parent or guardian before investigating a complaint from a child. Complaints can also be made by voluntary bodies like NAYPIC on young people's behalf. Children would always be interviewed 'if of appropriate age', unless there were special reasons (eg medical) not to do so.

In Scotland, the Commission was established by the Local Government (Scotland) Act 1975. While some complaints have involved under-18s, without exception they have been made by parents, generally on their own behalf.

In Northern Ireland, the Commissioner for Complaints was set up by the Commissioner for Complaints Act 1969, since amended, with similar functions five years before the Commissioners for Local Administration. Customarily the same person acts as Parliamentary Commissioner for Administration in Northern Ireland. No age-based records are kept of complaints, but it is clear there have been very few by under-18s; some complaints have been made by parents on educational matters. There are no special arrangements for complaints from children and young people. There are distinctive arrangements in Northern Ireland for pursuing findings of maladministration. If unable to effect a settlement, the Commissioner for Complaints issues a report to the complainant setting out the findings of maladministration. The complainant can then go the county court which will determine compensation.

Police Complaints Authority

The Authority was set up under the Police and Criminal Evidence Act 1984 to supervise investigations into the most serious complaints, and to review the reports of every investigation, whether supervised by the Authority or not, to decide whether disciplinary charges should be brought against officers concerned, if it is not already the intention of the relevant chief officer to do so. In 1989 the Authority was supervising the investigation of almost 800 cases and reviewed over 5,000 cases during the year. No statistical record is kept of the ages of complainants. There are no special arrangements for dealing with complaints from under-18s.

Equal Opportunities Commission

The EOC was set up by the Sex Discrimination Act 1975. It handles individual complaints relating to employment, goods, facilities, services and education. Complaints from parents and children constitute approximately 2-5% of the total. No special steps are taken to encourage under-18s to use the Commission for pursuing complaints. Individual complaints concerning schooling are recorded, usually from parents on behalf of children. Topics of recent complaints (approximately 100 in 1990) include access to curriculum subjects, access to schools, banding and streaming within schools, school uniform and work placements. Most complaints are resolved by negotiation, but some are not resolved. The EOC states that the 'complexity and lengthiness' of county court proceedings inhibits legal action by parents.

Commission for Racial Equality

The CRE was set up under the Race Relations Act 1976. Complaints of racial discrimination affecting children or young people are mostly education-related and constitute less than 5% of the total number of complaints. Some complaints are received directly from children. Some recent complaints involving children and young people have concerned racial harassment, exclusion from school, school admissions and trans-racial fostering and adoption.

Mental Health Act Commission

The Commission was established under the Mental Health Act 1983 to perform various functions to safeguard the rights of patients detained under the Act, including investigating complaints. There is no lower age limit on detention under the Act, but in fact very few under-18s are formally detained - most under-18s in mental hospitals are informal patients admitted by their parents. The Commission has sought to have its remit extended to cover informal patients. Very few complaints are received from or on behalf of under-18s and no special steps are taken to encourage them to use the Commission.

Responses to Survey

We received replies to our survey from the following bodies:

Advertising Standards Authority
Air Transport Users' Committee
Association of Community Health Councils of England and Wales
Banking Ombudsman
Broadcasting Complaints Commission

Building Societies Ombudsman
Central Transport Consultative Committee
Commissioners for Local Administration in England, Wales and Scotland
Commission for Racial Equality
Council on Tribunals
Data Protection Registrar
Equal Opportunities Commission
General Consumer Council for Northern Ireland
General Medical Council
Health and Safety Executive
Health Service Commissioner
Mental Health Act Commission
National Association of Citizens' Advice Bureaux
Northern Ireland Commissioner for Complaints
Office of Fair Trading
Office of Gas Supply
Office of Telecommunications
Office of the Lay Observer (Scotland)
Office of Water Services
Official Solicitor's Department
Parliamentary Commissioner for Administration
Police Complaints Authority
Solicitors' Complaints Bureau

Good Practice for Complaints Procedures

Appendix 4

The Commissioner could promote the following as principles of good practice for the use of complaints procedures by children and young people. They are not a complete set of criteria[1] for assessing the suitability of procedures but rather a number of points which apply particularly to children and young people, and some of course would also apply to adults. It is important that complaints procedures work effectively for children and young people, since they are particularly vulnerable and are also likely to be comparatively apprehensive about making complaints.

1. The rights of children and young people and the procedures for complaint if these rights are disregarded should be well-publicised to children and young people through appropriate media. Where the procedures are also used by adults consideration should be given to ways of specifically publicising their availability to children and young people, eg special leaflets or issuing special reports on their use by children and young people.
2. The procedures should be accessible to children and young people. Depending on the nature of the procedure, this might involve opening hours or telephone hours which are convenient to children, a freephone system and use of reply-paid envelopes or a freepost address, given the lack in children's resources. It might also involve the use of simple forms and allowing complaints by phone or in person rather than in writing. It should be as local as possible. Where the procedure is also used by adults it may be appropriate to publicise the name of a particular officer for handling complaints from children and young people. Officers who receive complaints should also be able to help children and young people who are often unaware whether their concern constitutes a 'complaint'.
3. Complaints should be accepted from children directly without requiring parental or other adult approval.
4. Parents or other adults, where this is in the child's best interests, should be able to make a complaint on behalf of a child, if a child who has sufficient understanding grants approval or if the child is unable to complain directly due to age or disability.
5. The procedure should be speedy, with possibly a fast track for children's complaints since they are likely to find delays more distressing than adults. The

complainant should be informed at every stage as to what is happening and should also be able to withdraw the complaint.

6. The procedure should be simple and user-friendly. For example where it is necessary to interview children this should be done if the children prefer on their own ground rather than requiring them to come to the offices of the investigating body. They should be allowed to have a friend or adviser present. Where appropriate, interviewers should be sensitive to the issues involved in interviewing young children or those with severe learning difficulties.

7. Where possible and appropriate, children and young people should have access to a free, easily accessible, independent and confidential advocacy service which could provide support, advice and assistance.

Notes

1. For wider criteria see for example Lynne Berry & Nick Doyle, *Open to Complaints: Guidelines for Social Services Complaints Procedures*, National Consumer Council/National Institute for Social Work, 1988.

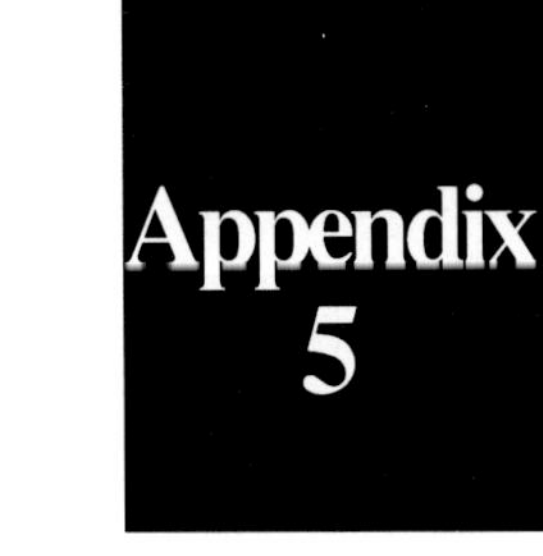

The United Nations Convention on the Rights of the Child

The Convention on the Rights of the Child was adopted by the United Nations General Assembly on 20 November, 1989. Its text is as follows.

THE CONVENTION ON THE RIGHTS OF THE CHILD

Adopted by the General Assembly of the United Nations on 20 November 1989

Text

PREAMBLE

The States Parties to the present Convention,

Considering that, in accordance with the principles proclaimed in the Charter of the United Nations, recognition of the inherent dignity and of the equal and inalienable rights of all members of the human family is the foundation of freedom, justice and peace in the world,

Bearing in mind that the peoples of the United Nations have, in the Charter, reaffirmed their faith in fundamental human rights and in the dignity and worth of the human person, and have determined to promote social progress and better standards of life in larger freedom,

Recognizing that the United Nations has, in the Universal Declaration of Human Rights and in the International Covenants on Human Rights, proclaimed and agreed that everyone is entitled to all the rights and freedoms set forth therein, without distinction of any kind, such as race, colour, sex, language, religion, political or other opinion, national or social origin, property, birth or other status,

Recalling that, in the Universal Declaration of Human Rights, the United Nations has proclaimed that childhood is entitled to special care and assistance,

Convinced that the family, as the fundamental group of society and the natural environment for the growth and well-being of all its members and particularly children, should be afforded the necessary protection and assistance so that it can fully assume its responsibilities within the community,

Recognizing that the child, for the full and harmonious development of his or her personality, should grow up in a family environment, in an atmosphere of happiness, love and understanding,

Considering that the child should be fully prepared to live an individual life in society, and brought up in the spirit of the ideals proclaimed in the Charter of the United Nations, and in particular in the spirit of peace, dignity, tolerance, freedom, equality and solidarity,

Bearing in mind that the need to extend particular care to the child has been stated in the Geneva Declaration of the Rights of the Child of 1924 and in the Declaration of the Rights of the Child adopted by the United Nations on 20 November 1959 and recognized in the Universal Declaration of Human Rights, in the International Covenant on Civil and Political Rights (in particular in articles 23 and 24), in the International Covenant on Economic, Social and Cultural Rights (in particular in article 10) and in the statutes and relevant instruments of specialized agencies and international organizations concerned with the welfare of children,

Bearing in mind that, as indicated in the Declaration of the Rights of the Child, "the child, by reason of his physical and mental immaturity, needs special safeguards and care, including appropriate legal protection, before as well as after birth",

Recalling the provisions of the Declaration on Social and Legal Principles relating to the Protection and Welfare of Children, with Special Reference to Foster Placement and Adoption Nationally and Internationally; the United Nations Standard Minimum Rules for the Administration of Juvenile Justice ("The Beijing Rules"); and the Declaration on the Protection of Women and Children in Emergency and Armed Conflict,

Recognizing that, in all countries in the world, there are children living in exceptionally difficult conditions, and that such children need special consideration,

Unofficial summary of main provisions

PREAMBLE

The preamble recalls the basic principles of the United Nations and specific provisions of certain relevant human rights treaties and proclamations. It reaffirms the fact that children, because of their vulnerability, need special care and protection, and it places special emphasis on the primary caring and protective responsibility of the family. It also reaffirms the need for legal and other protection of the child before and after birth, the importance of respect for the cultural values of the child's community, and the vital role of international cooperation in securing children's rights.

THE CONVENTION ON THE RIGHTS OF THE CHILD

Text

Taking due account of the importance of the traditions and cultural values of each people for the protection and harmonious development of the child,

Recognizing the importance of international co-operation for improving the living conditions of children in every country, in particular in the developing countries,

Have agreed as follows:

PART I

Article 1

For the purposes of the present Convention, a child means every human being below the age of 18 years unless, under the law applicable to the child, majority is attained earlier.

Article 2

1. States Parties shall respect and ensure the rights set forth in the present Convention to each child within their jurisdiction without discrimination of any kind, irrespective of the child's or his or her parent's or legal guardian's race, colour, sex, language, religion, political or other opinion, national, ethnic or social origin, property, disability, birth or other status.

2. States Parties shall take all appropriate measures to ensure that the child is protected against all forms of discrimination or punishment on the basis of the status, activities, expressed opinions, or beliefs of the child's parents, legal guardians, or family members.

Article 3

1. In all actions concerning children, whether undertaken by public or private social welfare institutions, courts of law, administrative authorities or legislative bodies, the best interests of the child shall be a primary consideration.

2. States Parties undertake to ensure the child such protection and care as is necessary for his or her well-being, taking into account the rights and duties of his or her parents, legal guardians, or other individuals legally responsible for him or her, and, to this end, shall take all appropriate legislative and administrative measures.

3. States Parties shall ensure that the institutions, services and facilities responsible for the care or protection of children shall conform with the standards established by competent authorities, particularly in the areas of safety, health, in the number and suitability of their staff, as well as competent supervision.

Article 4

States Parties shall undertake all appropriate legislative, administrative, and other measures for the implementation of the rights recognized in the present Convention. With regard to economic, social and cultural rights, States Parties shall undertake such measures to the maximum extent of their available resources and, where needed, within the framework of international co-operation.

Unofficial summary of main provisions

Definition of a child

A child is recognized as a person under 18, unless national laws recognize the age of majority earlier.

Non-discrimination

All rights apply to all children without exception. It is the State's obligation to protect children from any form of discrimination and to take positive action to promote their rights.

Best interests of the child

All actions concerning the child shall take full account of his or her best interests. The State shall provide the child with adequate care when parents, or others charged with that responsibility, fail to do so.

Implementation of rights

The State must do all it can to implement the rights contained in the Convention.

THE CONVENTION ON THE RIGHTS OF THE CHILD

Text

Article 5

States Parties shall respect the responsibilities, rights and duties of parents or, where applicable, the members of the extended family or community as provided for by local custom, legal guardians or other persons legally responsible for the child, to provide, in a manner consistent with the evolving capacities of the child, appropriate direction and guidance in the exercise by the child of the rights recognized in the present Convention.

Article 6

1. States Parties recognize that every child has the inherent right to life.

2. States Parties shall ensure to the maximum extent possible the survival and development of the child.

Article 7

1. The child shall be registered immediately after birth and shall have the right from birth to a name, the right to acquire a nationality and, as far as possible, the right to know and be cared for by his or her parents.

2. States Parties shall ensure the implementation of these rights in accordance with their national law and their obligations under the relevant international instruments in this field, in particular where the child would otherwise be stateless.

Article 8

1. States Parties undertake to respect the right of the child to preserve his or her identity, including nationality, name and family relations as recognized by law without unlawful interference.

2. Where a child is illegally deprived of some or all of the elements of his or her identity, States Parties shall provide appropriate assistance and protection, with a view to speedily re-establishing his or her identity.

Article 9

1. States Parties shall ensure that a child shall not be separated from his or her parents against their will, except when competent authorities subject to judicial review determine, in accordance with applicable law and procedures, that such separation is necessary for the best interests of the child. Such determination may be necessary in a particular case such as one involving abuse or neglect of the child by the parents, or one where the parents are living separately and a decision must be made as to the child's place of residence.

2. In any proceedings pursuant to paragraph 1 of the present article, all interested parties shall be given an opportunity to participate in the proceedings and make their views known.

3. States Parties shall respect the right of the child who is separated from one or both parents to maintain personal relations and direct contact with both parents on a regular basis, except if it is contrary to the child's best interests.

4. Where such separation results from any action initiated by a State Party, such as the detention, imprisonment, exile, deportation or death (including death arising from any cause while the person is in the custody of the State) of one or both parents or of the child, that State Party shall, upon request, provide the parents, the child or, if appropriate, another member of the family with the essential information concerning the whereabouts of the absent member(s) of the family unless the provision of the information would be detrimental to the well-being of the child. States Parties shall further ensure that the submission of such a request shall of itself entail no adverse consequences for the person(s) concerned.

Unofficial summary of main provisions

Parental guidance and the child's evolving capacities

The State must respect the rights and responsibilities of parents and the extended family to provide guidance for the child which is appropriate to her or his evolving capacities.

Survival and development

Every child has the inherent right to life, and the State has an obligation to ensure the child's survival and development.

Name and nationality

The child has the right to a name at birth. The child also has the right to acquire a nationality and, as far as possible, to know his or her parents and be cared for by them.

Preservation of identity

The State has an obligation to protect, and if necessary, re-establish basic aspects of the child's identity. This includes name, nationality and family ties.

Separation from parents

The child has a right to live with his or her parents unless this is deemed to be incompatible with the child's best interests. The child also has the right to maintain contact with both parents if separated from one or both.

Text

Unofficial summary of main provisions

Article 10

1. In accordance with the obligation of States Parties under article 9, paragraph 1, applications by a child or his or her parents to enter or leave a State Party for the purpose of family reunification shall be dealt with by States Parties in a positive, humane and expeditious manner. States Parties shall further ensure that the submission of such a request shall entail no adverse consequences for the applicants and for the members of their family.

2. A child whose parents reside in different States shall have the right to maintain on a regular basis, save in exceptional circumstances personal relations and direct contacts with both parents. Towards that end and in accordance with the obligation of States Parties under article 9, paragraph 1, States Parties shall respect the right of the child and his or her parents to leave any country, including their own, and to enter their own country. The right to leave any country shall be subject only to such restrictions as are prescribed by law and which are necessary to protect the national security, public order *(ordre public),* public health or morals or the rights and freedoms of others and are consistent with the other rights recognized in the present Convention.

Family reunification

Children and their parents have the right to leave any country and to enter their own for purposes of reunion or the maintenance of the child-parent relationship.

Article 11

1. States Parties shall take measures to combat the illicit transfer and non-return of children abroad.

2. To this end, States Parties shall promote the conclusion of bilateral or multilateral agreements or accession to existing agreements.

Illicit transfer and non-return

The State has an obligation to prevent and remedy the kidnapping or retention of children abroad by a parent or third party.

Article 12

1. States Parties shall assure to the child who is capable of forming his or her own views the right to express those views freely in all matters affecting the child, the views of the child being given due weight in accordance with the age and maturity of the child.

2. For this purpose, the child shall in particular be provided the opportunity to be heard in any judicial and administrative proceedings affecting the child, either directly, or through a representative or an appropriate body, in a manner consistent with the procedural rules of national law.

The child's opinion

The child has the right to express his or her opinion freely and to have that opinion taken into account in any matter or procedure affecting the child.

Article 13

1. The child shall have the right to freedom of expression; this right shall include freedom to seek, receive and impart information and ideas of all kinds, regardless of frontiers, either orally, in writing or in print, in the form of art, or through any other media of the child's choice.

2. The exercise of this right may be subject to certain restrictions, but these shall only be such as are provided by law and are necessary:

(a) For respect of the rights or reputations of others; or

(b) For the protection of national security or of public order *(ordre public),* or of public health or morals.

Freedom of expression

The child has the right to express his or her views, obtain information, make ideas or information known, regardless of frontiers.

Article 14

1. States Parties shall respect the right of the child to freedom of thought, conscience and religion.

2. States Parties shall respect the rights and duties of the parents and, when applicable, legal guardians, to provide direction to the child in the exercise of his or her right in a manner consistent with the evolving capacities of the child.

Freedom of thought, conscience and religion

The State shall respect the child's right to freedom of thought, conscience and religion, subject to appropriate parental guidance.

THE CONVENTION ON THE RIGHTS OF THE CHILD

Text

Unofficial summary of main provisions

3. Freedom to manifest one's religion or beliefs may be subject only to such limitations as are prescribed by law and are necessary to protect public safety, order, health or morals, or the fundamental rights and freedoms of others.

Article 15

1. States Parties recognize the rights of the child to freedom of association and to freedom of peaceful assembly.

2. No restrictions may be placed on the exercise of these rights other than those imposed in conformity with the law and which are necessary in a democratic society in the interests of national security or public safety, public order *(ordre public)*, the protection of public health or morals or the protection of the rights and freedoms of others.

Freedom of association

Children have a right to meet with others, and to join or form associations.

Article16

1. No child shall be subjected to arbitrary or unlawful interference with his or her privacy, family, home or correspondence, nor to unlawful attacks on his or her honour and reputation.

2. The child has the right to the protection of the law against such interference or attacks.

Protection of privacy

Children have the right to protection from interference with privacy, family, home and correspondence, and from libel or slander.

Article 17

States Parties recognize the important function performed by the mass media and shall ensure that the child has access to information and material from a diversity of national and international sources, especially those aimed at the promotion of his or her social, spiritual and moral well-being and physical and mental health. To this end, States Parties shall:

(a) Encourage the mass media to disseminate information and material of social and cultural benefit to the child and in accordance with the spirit of article 29;

(b) Encourage international co-operation in the production, exchange and dissemination of such information and material from a diversity of cultural, national and international sources;

(c) Encourage the production and dissemination of children's books;

(d) Encourage the mass media to have particular regard to the linguistic needs of the child who belongs to a minority group or who is indigenous;

(e) Encourage the development of appropriate guidelines for the protection of the child from information and material injurious to his or her well-being, bearing in mind the provisions of articles 13 and 18.

Access to appropriate information

The State shall ensure the accessibility to children of information and material from a diversity of sources, and it shall encourage the mass media to disseminate information which is of social and cultural benefit to the child, and take steps to protect him or her from harmful materials.

Article 18

1. States Parties shall use their best efforts to ensure recognition of the principle that both parents have common responsibilities for the upbringing and development of the child. Parents or, as the case may be, legal guardians, have the primary responsibility for the upbringing and development of the child. The best interests of the child will be their basic concern.

2. For the purpose of guaranteeing and promoting the rights set forth in the present Convention, States Parties shall render appropriate assistance to parents and legal guardians in the performance of their child-rearing responsibilities and shall ensure the development of institutions, facilities and services for the care of children.

3. States Parties shall take all appropriate measures to ensure that children of working parents have the right to benefit from child-care services and facilities for which they are eligible.

Parental responsibilities

Parents have joint primary responsibility for raising the child, and the State shall support them in this. The State shall provide appropriate assistance to parents in child-raising.

Text

Article 19

1. States Parties shall take all appropriate legislative, administrative, social and educational measures to protect the child from all forms of physical or mental violence, injury or abuse, neglect or negligent treatment, maltreatment or exploitation, including sexual abuse, while in the care of parent(s), legal guardian(s) or any other person who has the care of the child.

2. Such protective measures should, as appropriate, include effective procedures for the establishment of social programmes to provide necessary support for the child and for those who have the care of the child, as well as for other forms of prevention and for identification, reporting, referral, investigation, treatment and follow-up of instances of child maltreatment described heretofore, and, as appropriate, for judicial involvement.

Article 20

1. A child temporarily or permanently deprived of his or her family environment, or in whose own best interests cannot be allowed to remain in that environment, shall be entitled to special protection and assistance provided by the State.

2. States Parties shall in accordance with their national laws ensure alternative care for such a child.

3. Such care could include, *inter alia,* foster placement, *Kafala* of Islamic law, adoption, or if necessary placement in suitable institutions for the care of children. When considering solutions, due regard shall be paid to the desirability of continuity in a child's upbringing and to the child's ethnic, religious, cultural and linguistic background.

Article 21

States Parties that recognize and/or permit the system of adoption shall ensure that the best interests of the child shall be the paramount consideration and they shall:

(a) Ensure that the adoption of a child is authorized only by competent authorities who determine, in accordance with applicable law and procedures and on the basis of all pertinent and reliable information, that the adoption is permissible in view of the child's status concerning parents, relatives and legal guardians and that, if required, the persons concerned have given their informed consent to the adoption on the basis of such counselling as may be necessary;

(b) Recognize that inter-country adoption may be considered as an alternative means of child's care, if the child cannot be placed in a foster or an adoptive family or cannot in any suitable manner be cared for in the child's country of origin;

(c) Ensure that the child concerned by intercountry adoption enjoys safeguards and standards equivalent to those existing in the case of national adoption;

(d) Take all appropriate measures to ensure that, in intercountry adoption, the placement does not result in improper financial gain for those involved in it;

(e) Promote, where appropriate, the objectives of the present article by concluding bilateral or multilateral arrangements or agreements, and endeavour, within this framework, to ensure that the placement of the child in another country is carried out by competent authorities or organs.

Unofficial summary of main provisions

Protection from abuse and neglect

The State shall protect the child from all forms of maltreatment by parents or others responsible for the care of the child and establish appropriate social programmes for the prevention of abuse and the treatment of victims.

Protection of a child without family

The State is obliged to provide special protection for a child deprived of the family environment and to ensure that appropriate alternative family care or institutional placement is available in such cases. Efforts to meet this obligation shall pay due regard to the child's cultural background.

Adoption

In countries where adoption is recognized and/or allowed, it shall only be carried out in the best interests of the child, and then only with the authorization of competent authorities, and safeguards for the child.

THE CONVENTION ON THE RIGHTS OF THE CHILD

Text

Article 22

1. States Parties shall take appropriate measures to ensure that a child who is seeking refugee status or who is considered a refugee in accordance with applicable international or domestic law and procedures shall, whether unaccompanied or accompanied by his or her parents or by any other person, receive appropriate protection and humanitarian assistance in the enjoyment of applicable rights set forth in the present Convention and in other international human rights or humanitarian instruments to which the said States are Parties.

2. For this purpose, States Parties shall provide, as they consider appropriate, co-operation in any efforts by the United Nations and other competent intergovernmental organizations or non-governmental organizations co-operating with the United Nations to protect and assist such a child and to trace the parents or other members of the family of any refugee child in order to obtain information necessary for reunification with his or her family. In cases where no parents or other members of the family can be found, the child shall be accorded the same protection as any other child permanently or temporarily deprived of his or her family environment for any reason, as set forth in the present Convention.

Article 23

1. States Parties recognize that a mentally or physically disabled child should enjoy a full and decent life, in conditions which ensure dignity, promote self-reliance, and facilitate the child's active participation in the community.

2. States Parties recognize the right of the disabled child to special care and shall encourage and ensure the extension, subject to available resources, to the eligible child and those responsible for his or her care, of assistance for which application is made and which is appropriate to the child's condition and to the circumstances of the parents or others caring for the child.

3. Recognizing the special needs of a disabled child, assistance extended in accordance with paragraph 2 of the present article shall be provided free of charge, whenever possible, taking into account the financial resources of the parents or others caring for the child, and shall be designed to ensure that the disabled child has effective access to and receives education, training, health care services, rehabilitation services, preparation for employment and recreation opportunities in a manner conducive to the child's achieving the fullest possible social integration and individual development, including his or her cultural and spiritual development.

4. States Parties shall promote, in the spirit of international co-operation, the exchange of appropriate information in the field of preventive health care and of medical, psychological and functional treatment of disabled children, including dissemination of and access to information concerning methods of rehabilitation, education and vocational services, with the aim of enabling States Parties to improve their capabilities and skills and to widen their experience in these areas. In this regard, particular account shall be taken of the needs of developing countries.

Article 24

1. States Parties recognize the right of the child to the enjoyment of the highest attainable standard of health and to facilities for the treatment of illness and rehabilitation of health. States Parties shall strive to ensure that no child is deprived of his or her right of access to such health care services.

2. States Parties shall pursue full implementation of this right and, in particular, shall take appropriate measures:

(a) To diminish infant and child mortality;

Unofficial summary of main provisions

Refugee children

Special protection shall be granted to a refugee child or to a child seeking refugee status. It is the State's obligation to co-operate with competent organizations which provide such protection and assistance.

Disabled children

A disabled child has the right to special care, education and training to help him or her enjoy a full and decent life in dignity and achieve the greatest degree of self-reliance and social integration possible.

Health and health services

The child has a right to the highest standard of health and medical care attainable. States shall place special emphasis on the provision of primary and preventive health care, public health education and the reduction of infant mortality. They shall encourage international co-operation in this regard and

Text

(b) To ensure the provision of necessary medical assistance and health care to all children with emphasis on the development of primary health care;

(c) To combat disease and malnutrition including within the framework of primary health care, through *inter alia* the application of readily available technology and through the provision of adequate nutritious foods and clean drinking water, taking into consideration the dangers and risks of environmental pollution;

(d) To ensure appropriate pre-natal and post-natal health care for mothers;

(e) To ensure that all segments of society, in particular parents and children, are informed, have access to education and are supported in the use of basic knowledge of child health and nutrition, the advantages of breast-feeding, hygiene and environmental sanitation and the prevention of accidents;

(f) To develop preventive health care, guidance for parents and family planning education and services.

3. States Parties shall take all effective and appropriate measures with a view to abolishing traditional practices prejudicial to the health of children.

4. States Parties undertake to promote and encourage international co-operation with a view to achieving progressively the full realization of the right recognized in the present article. In this regard, particular account shall be taken of the needs of developing countries.

Article 25

States Parties recognize the right of a child who has been placed by the competent authorities for the purposes of care, protection or treatment of his or her physical or mental health, to a periodic review of the treatment provided to the child and all other circumstances relevant to his or her placement.

Article 26

1. States Parties shall recognize for every child the right to benefit from social security, including social insurance, and shall take the necessary measures to achieve the full realization of this right in accordance with their national law.

2. The benefits should, where appropriate, be granted, taking into account the resources and the circumstances of the child and persons having responsibility for the maintenance of the child, as well as any other consideration relevant to an application for benefits made by or on behalf of the child.

Article 27

1. States Parties recognize the right of every child to a standard of living adequate for the child's physical, mental, spiritual, moral and social development.

2. The parent(s) or others responsible for the child have the primary responsibility to secure, within their abilities and financial capacities, the conditions of living necessary for the child's development.

3. States Parties, in accordance with national conditions and within their means, shall take appropriate measures to assist parents and others responsible for the child to implement this right and shall in case of need provide material assistance and support programmes, particularly with regard to nutrition, clothing and housing.

4. States Parties shall take all appropriate measures to secure the recovery of maintenance for the child from the parents or other persons having financial responsibility for the child, both within the State Party and from abroad. In particular, where the person having financial responsibility for the child lives in a State different from that of the child, States Parties shall promote the accession to international agreements or the conclusion of such agreements, as well as the making of other appropriate arrangements.

Unofficial summary of main provisions

Health and health services (continued)

strive to see that no child is deprived of access to effective health services.

Periodic review of placement

A child who is placed by the State for reasons of care, protection or treatment is entitled to have that placement evaluated regularly.

Social security

The child has the right to benefit from social security including social insurance.

Standard of living

Every child has the right to a standard of living adequate for his or her physical, mental, spiritual, moral and social development. Parents have the primary responsibility to ensure that the child has an adequate standard of living. The State's duty is to ensure that this responsibility can be fulfilled, and is. State responsibility can include material assistance to parents and their children.

THE CONVENTION ON THE RIGHTS OF THE CHILD

Text

Article 28

1. States Parties recognize the right of the child to education, and with a view to achieving this right progressively and on the basis of equal opportunity, they shall, in particular:

(a) Make primary education compulsory and available free to all;

(b) Encourage the development of different forms of secondary education, including general and vocational education, make them available and accessible to every child, and take appropriate measures such as the introduction of free education and offering financial assistance in case of need;

(c) Make higher education accessible to all on the basis of capacity by every appropriate means;

(d) Make educational and vocational information and guidance available and accessible to all children;

(e) Take measures to encourage regular attendance at schools and the reduction of drop-out rates.

2. States Parties shall take all appropriate measures to ensure that school discipline is administered in a manner consistent with the child's human dignity and in conformity with the present Convention.

3. States Parties shall promote and encourage international co-operation in matters relating to education, in particular with a view to contributing to the elimination of ignorance and illiteracy throughout the world and facilitating access to scientific and technical knowledge and modern teaching methods. In this regard, particular account shall be taken of the needs of developing countries.

Article 29

1. States Parties agree that the education of the child shall be directed to:

(a) The development of the child's personality, talents and mental and physical abilities to their fullest potential;

(b) The development of respect for human rights and fundamental freedoms, and for the principles enshrined in the Charter of the United Nations;

(c) The development of respect for the child's parents, his or her own cultural identity, language and values, for the national values of the country in which the child is living, the country from which he or she may originate, and for civilizations different from his or her own;

(d) The preparation of the child for responsible life in a free society, in the spirit of understanding, peace, tolerance, equality of sexes, and friendship among all peoples, ethnic, national and religious groups and persons of indigenous origin;

(e) The development of respect for the natural environment.

2. No part of the present article or article 28 shall be construed so as to interfere with the liberty of individuals and bodies to establish and direct educational institutions, subject always to the observance of the principles set forth in paragraph 1 of the present article and to the requirements that the education given in such institutions shall conform to such minimum standards as may be laid down by the State.

Article 30

In those States in which ethnic, religious or linguistic minorities or persons of indigenous origin exist, a child belonging to such a minority or who is indigenous shall not be denied the right, in community with other members of his or her group, to enjoy his or her own culture, to profess and practise his or her own religion, or to use his or her own language.

Unofficial summary of main provisions

Education

The child has a right to education, and the State's duty is to ensure that primary education is free and compulsory, to encourage different forms of secondary education accessible to every child and to make higher education available to all on the basis of capacity. School discipline shall be consistent with the child's rights and dignity. The State shall engage in international co-operation to implement this right.

Aims of education

Education shall aim at developing the child's personality, talents and mental and physical abilities to the fullest extent. Education shall prepare the child for an active adult life in a free society and foster respect for the child's parents, his or her own cultural identity, language and values, and for the cultural background and values of others.

Children of minorities or indigenous populations

Children of minority communities and indigenous populations have the right to enjoy their own culture and to practise their own religion and language.

Text

Article 31

1. States Parties recognize the right of the child to rest and leisure, to engage in play and recreational activities appropriate to the age of the child and to participate freely in cultural life and the arts.

2. States Parties shall respect and promote the right of the child to participate fully in cultural and artistic life and shall encourage the provision of appropriate and equal opportunities for cultural, artistic, recreational and leisure activity.

Article 32

1. States Parties recognize the right of the child to be protected from economic exploitation and from performing any work that is likely to be hazardous or to interfere with the child's education, or to be harmful to the child's health or physical, mental, spiritual, moral or social development.

2. States Parties shall take legislative, administrative, social and educational measures to ensure the implementation of the present article. To this end, and having regard to the relevant provisions of other international instruments, States Parties shall in particular:

(a) Provide for a minimum age or minimum ages for admissions to employment;

(b) Provide for appropriate regulation of the hours and conditions of employment;

(c) Provide for appropriate penalties or other sanctions to ensure the effective enforcement of the present article.

Article 33

States Parties shall take all appropriate measures, including legislative, administrative, social and educational measures, to protect children from the illicit use of narcotic drugs and psychotropic substances as defined in the relevant international treaties, and to prevent the use of children in the illicit production and trafficking of such substances.

Article 34

States Parties undertake to protect the child from all forms of sexual exploitation and sexual abuse. For these purposes, States Parties shall in particular take all appropriate national, bilateral and multilateral measures to prevent:

(a) The inducement or coercion of a child to engage in any unlawful sexual activity;

(b) The exploitative use of children in prostitution or other unlawful sexual practices;

(c) The exploitative use of children in pornographic performances and materials.

Article 35

States Parties shall take all appropriate national, bilateral and multilateral measures to prevent the abduction of, the sale of or traffic in children for any purpose or in any form.

Article 36

States Parties shall protect the child against all other forms of exploitation prejudicial to any aspects of the child's welfare.

Unofficial summary of main provisions

Leisure, recreation and cultural activities

The child has the right to leisure, play and participation in cultural and artistic activities.

Child labour

The child has the right to be protected from work that threatens his or her health, education or development. The State shall set minimum ages for employment and regulate working conditions.

Drug abuse

Children have the right to protection from the use of narcotic and psychotropic drugs, and from being involved in their production or distribution.

Sexual exploitation

The State shall protect children from sexual exploitation and abuse, including prostitution and involvement in pornography.

Sale, trafficking and abduction

It is the State's obligation to make every effort to prevent the sale, trafficking and abduction of children.

Other forms of exploitation

The child has the right to protection from all forms of exploitation prejudicial to any aspects of the child's welfare not covered in articles 32, 33, 34 and 35.

THE CONVENTION ON THE RIGHTS OF THE CHILD

Text

Article 37

States Parties shall ensure that:

(a) No child shall be subjected to torture or other cruel, inhuman or degrading treatment or punishment. Neither capital punishment nor life imprisonment without possibility of release shall be imposed for offences committed by persons below 18 years of age;

(b) No child shall be deprived of his or her liberty unlawfully or arbitrarily. The arrest, detention or imprisonment of a child shall be in conformity with the law and shall be used only as a measure of last resort and for the shortest appropriate period of time;

(c) Every child deprived of liberty shall be treated with humanity and respect for the inherent dignity of the human person, and in a manner which takes into account the needs of persons of his or her age. In particular every child deprived of liberty shall be separated from adults unless it is considered in the child's best interest not to do so and shall have the right to maintain contact with his or her family through correspondence and visits, save in exceptional circumstances;

(d) Every child deprived of his or her liberty shall have the right to prompt access to legal and other appropriate assistance, as well as the right to challenge the legality of the deprivation of his or her liberty before a court or other competent, independent and impartial authority, and to a prompt decision on any such action.

Article 38

1. States Parties undertake to respect and to ensure respect for rules of international humanitarian law applicable to them in armed conflicts which are relevant to the child.

2. States Parties shall take all feasible measures to ensure that persons who have not attained the age of 15 years do not take a direct part in hostilities.

3. States Parties shall refrain from recruiting any person who has not attained the age of 15 years into their armed forces. In recruiting among those persons who have attained the age of 15 years but who have not attained the age of 18 years, States Parties shall endeavour to give priority to those who are oldest.

4. In accordance with their obligations under international humanitarian law to protect the civilian population in armed conflicts, States Parties shall take all feasible measures to ensure protection and care of children who are affected by an armed conflict.

Article 39

States Parties shall take all appropriate measures to promote physical and psychological recovery and social reintegration of a child victim of: any form of neglect, exploitation, or abuse; torture or any other form of cruel, inhuman or degrading treatment or punishment; or armed conflicts. Such recovery and reintegration shall take place in an environment which fosters the health, self-respect and dignity of the child.

Article 40

1. States Parties recognize the right of every child alleged as, accused of, or recognized as having infringed the penal law to be treated in a manner consistent with the promotion of the child's sense of dignity and worth, which reinforces the child's respect for the human rights and fundamental freedoms of others and which takes into account the child's age and the desirability of promoting the child's reintegration and the child's assuming a constructive role in society.

Unofficial summary of main provisions

Torture and deprivation of liberty

No child shall be subjected to torture, cruel treatment or punishment, unlawful arrest or deprivation of liberty. Both capital punishment and life imprisonment without the possibility of release are prohibited for offences committed by persons below 18 years. Any child deprived of liberty shall be separated from adults unless it is considered in the child's best interests not to do so. A child who is detained shall have legal and other assistance as well as contact with the family.

Armed conflicts

States Parties shall take all feasible measures to ensure that children under 15 years of age have no direct part in hostilities. No child below 15 shall be recruited into the armed forces. States shall also ensure the protection and care of children who are affected by armed conflict as described in relevant international law.

Rehabilitative care

The State has an obligation to ensure that child victims of armed conflicts, torture, neglect, maltreatment or exploitation receive appropriate treatment for their recovery and social reintegration.

Administration of juvenile justice

A child in conflict with the law has the right to treatment which promotes the child's sense of dignity and worth, takes the child's age into account and aims at his or her reintegration into society. The child is entitled to basic guarantees as well as legal or other assistance for his

Text

2. To this end, and having regard to the relevant provisions of international instruments, States Parties shall, in particular, ensure that:

(a) No child shall be alleged as, be accused of, or recognized as having infringed the penal law by reason of acts or omissions that were not prohibited by national or international law at the time they were committed;

(b) Every child alleged as or accused of having infringed the penal law has at least the following guarantees:

- *(i)* To be presumed innocent until proven guilty according to law;
- *(ii)* To be informed promptly and directly of the charges against him or her, and, if appropriate, through his or her parents or legal guardians, and to have legal or other appropriate assistance in the preparation and presentation of his or her defence;
- *(iii)* To have the matter determined without delay by a competent, independent and impartial authority or judicial body in a fair hearing according to law, in the presence of legal or other appropriate assistance and, unless it is considered not to be in the best interest of the child, in particular, taking into account his or her age or situation, his or her parents or legal guardians;
- *(iv)* Not to be compelled to give testimony or to confess guilt; to examine or have examined adverse witnesses and to obtain the participation and examination of witnesses on his or her behalf under conditions of equality;
- *(v)* If considered to have infringed the penal law, to have this decision and any measures imposed in consequence thereof reviewed by a higher competent, independent and impartial authority or judicial body according to law;
- *(vi)* To have the free assistance of an interpreter if the child cannot understand or speak the language used;
- *(vii)* To have his or her privacy fully respected at all stages of the proceedings.

3. States Parties shall seek to promote the establishment of laws, procedures, authorities and institutions specifically applicable to children alleged as, accused of, or recognized as having infringed the penal law, and, in particular:

(a) the establishment of a minimum age below which children shall be presumed not to have the capacity to infringe the penal law;

(b) whenever appropriate and desirable, measures for dealing with such children without resorting to judicial proceedings, providing that human rights and legal safeguards are fully respected.

4. A variety of dispositions, such as care, guidance and supervision orders; counselling; probation; foster care; education and vocational training programmes and other alternatives to institutional care shall be available to ensure that children are dealt with in a manner appropriate to their well-being and proportionate both to their circumstances and the offence.

Article 41

Nothing in the present Convention shall affect any provisions which are more conducive to the realization of the rights of the child and which may be contained in:

(a) The law of a State Party; or

(b) International law in force for that State.

Unofficial summary of main provisions

Administration of juvenile justice (continued)

or her defence. Judicial proceedings and institutional placements shall be avoided wherever possible.

Respect for higher standards

Wherever standards set in applicable national and international law relevant to the rights of the child that are higher than those in this Convention, the higher standard shall always apply.

THE CONVENTION ON THE RIGHTS OF THE CHILD

Text

PART II

Article 42

States Parties undertake to make the principles and provisions of the Convention widely known, by appropriate and active means, to adults and children alike.

Article 43

1. For the purpose of examining the progress made by States Parties in achieving the realization of the obligations undertaken in the present Convention, there shall be established a Committee on the Rights of the Child, which shall carry out the functions hereinafter provided.

2. The Committee shall consist of ten experts of high moral standing and recognized competence in the field covered by this Convention. The members of the Committee shall be elected by States Parties from among their nationals and shall serve in their personal capacity, consideration being given to equitable geographical distribution, as well as to the principal legal systems.

3. The members of the Committee shall be elected by secret ballot from a list of persons nominated by States Parties. Each State Party may nominate one person from among its own nationals.

4. The initial election to the Committee shall be held no later than six months after the date of the entry into force of the present Convention and thereafter every second year. At least four months before the date of each election, the Secretary-General of the United Nations shall address a letter to States Parties inviting them to submit their nominations within two months. The Secretary-General shall subsequently prepare a list in alphabetical order of all persons thus nominated, indicating States Parties which have nominated them, and shall submit it to the States Parties to the present Convention.

5. The elections shall be held at meetings of States Parties convened by the Secretary-General at United Nations Headquarters. At those meetings, for which two thirds of States Parties shall constitute a quorum, the persons elected to the Committee shall be those who obtain the largest number of votes and an absolute majority of the votes of the representatives of States Parties present and voting.

6. The members of the Committee shall be elected for a term of four years. They shall be eligible for re-election if renominated. The term of five of the members elected at the first election shall expire at the end of two years; immediately after the first election, the names of these five members shall be chosen by lot by the Chairman of the meeting.

7. If a member of the Committee dies or resigns or declares that for any other cause he or she can no longer perform the duties of the Committee, the State Party which nominated the member shall appoint another expert from among its nationals to serve for the remainder of the term, subject to the approval of the Committee.

8. The Committee shall establish its own rules of procedure.

9. The Committee shall elect its officers for a period of two years.

10. The meetings of the Committee shall normally be held at United Nations Headquarters or at any other convenient place as determined by the Committee. The Committee shall normally meet annually. The duration of the meetings of the Committee shall be determined, and reviewed, if necessary, by a meeting of the States Parties to the present Convention, subject to the approval of the General Assembly.

Unofficial summary of main provisions

Implementation and entry into force

The provisions of articles 42 - 54 notably foresee:

(i) *the State's obligation to make the rights contained in this Convention widely known to both adults and children.*

(ii) *the setting up of a Committee on the Rights of the child composed of ten experts, which will consider reports that States Parties to the Convention are to submit two years after ratification and every five years thereafter. The Convention enters into force—and the Committee would therefore be set up—once 20 countries have ratified it.*

(iii) *States Parties are to make their reports widely available to the general public.*

(iv) *The Committee may propose that special studies be undertaken on specific issues relating to the rights of the child, and may make its evaluations known to each State Party concerned as well as to the UN General Assembly.*

(v) *In order to "foster the effective implementation of the Convention and to encourage international cooperation", the specialized agencies of the UN (such as the ILO, WHO, and UNESCO) and UNICEF would be able to attend the meetings of the Committee. Together with any other body recognized as "competent", including NGOs in consultative status with the UN and UN organs such as the UNHCR, they can submit pertinent information to the Committee and be asked to advise on the optimal implementation of the Convention.*

11. The Secretary-General of the United Nations shall provide the necessary staff and facilities for the effective performance of the functions of the Committee under the present Convention.

12. With the approval of the General Assembly, the members of the Committee established under the present Convention shall receive emoluments from the United Nations resources on such terms and conditions as the Assembly may decide.

Article 44

1. States Parties undertake to submit to the Committee, through the Secretary-General of the United Nations, reports on the measures they have adopted which give effect to the rights recognized herein and on the progress made on the enjoyment of those rights:

(a) Within two years of the entry into force of the Convention for the State Party concerned,

(b) Thereafter every five years.

2. Reports made under the present article shall indicate factors and difficulties, if any, affecting the degree of fulfilment of the obligations under the present Convention. Reports shall also contain sufficient information to provide the Committee with a comprehensive understanding of the implementation of the Convention in the country concerned.

3. A State Party which has submitted a comprehensive initial report to the Committee need not in its subsequent reports submitted in accordance with paragraph 1 *(b)* of the present article repeat basic information previously provided.

4. The Committee may request from States Parties further information relevant to the implementation of the Convention.

5. The Committee shall submit to the General Assembly, through the Economic and Social Council, every two years, reports on its activities.

6. States Parties shall make their reports widely available to the public in their own countries.

Article 45

In order to foster the effective implementation of the Convention and to encourage international co-operation in the field covered by the Convention:

(a) The specialized agencies, the United Nations Children's Fund and other United Nations organs shall be entitled to be represented at the consideration of the implementation of such provisions of the present Convention as fall within the scope of their mandate. The Committee may invite the specialized agencies, the United Nations Children's Fund and other competent bodies as it may consider appropriate to provide expert advice on the implementation of the Convention in areas falling within the scope of their respective mandates. The Committee may invite the specialized agencies, the United Nations Children's Fund and other United Nations organs to submit reports on the implementation of the Convention in areas falling within the scope of their activities;

(b) The Committee shall transmit, as it may consider appropriate, to the specialized agencies, the United Nations Children's Fund and other competent bodies, any reports from States Parties that contain a request, or indicate a need, for technical advice or assistance, along with the Committee's observations and suggestions, if any, on these requests or indications;

(c) The Committee may recommend to the General Assembly to request the

THE CONVENTION ON THE RIGHTS OF THE CHILD

Text

Secretary-General to undertake on its behalf studies on specific issues relating to the rights of the child;

(d) The Committee may make suggestions and general recommendations based on information received pursuant to articles 44 and 45 of the present Convention. Such suggestions and general recommendations shall be transmitted to any State Party concerned and reported to the General Assembly, together with comments, if any, from States Parties.

PART III

Article 46

The present Convention shall be open for signature by all States.

Article 47

The present Convention is subject to ratification. Instruments of ratification shall be deposited with the Secretary-General of the United Nations.

Article 48

The present Convention shall remain open for accession by any State. The instruments of accession shall be deposited with the Secretary-General of the United Nations.

Article 49

1. The present Convention shall enter into force on the thirtieth day following the date of deposit with the Secretary-General of the United Nations of the twentieth instrument of ratification or accession.

2. For each State ratifying or acceding to the Convention after the deposit of the twentieth instrument of ratification or accession, the Convention shall enter into force on the thirtieth day after the deposit by such State of its instrument of ratification or accession.

Article 50

1. Any State Party may propose an amendment and file it with the Secretary-General of the United Nations. The Secretary-General shall thereupon communicate the proposed amendment to States Parties, with a request that they indicate whether they favour a conference of States Parties for the purpose of considering and voting upon the proposals. In the event that, within four months from the date of such communication, at least one third of the States Parties favour such a conference, the Secretary-General shall convene the conference under the auspices of the United Nations. Any amendment adopted by a majority of States Parties present and voting at the conference shall be submitted to the General Assembly for approval.

2. An amendment adopted in accordance with paragraph 1 of the present article shall enter into force when it has been approved by the General Assembly of the United Nations and accepted by a two-thirds majority of States Parties.

3. When an amendment enters into force, it shall be binding on those States Parties which have accepted it, other States Parties still being bound by the provisions of the present Convention and any earlier amendments which they have accepted.

Article 51

1. The Secretary-General of the United Nations shall receive and circulate to all States the text of reservations made by States at the time of ratification or accession.

2. A reservation incompatible with the object and purpose of the present Convention shall not be permitted.

3. Reservations may be withdrawn at any time by notification to that effect addressed to the Secretary-General of the United Nations, who shall then inform all States. Such notification shall take effect on the date on which it is received by the Secretary-General.

Article 52

A State Party may denounce the present Convention by written notification to the Secretary-General of the United Nations. Denunciation becomes effective one year after the date of receipt of the notification by the Secretary-General.

Article 53

The Secretary-General of the United Nations is designated as the depositary of the present Convention.

Article 54

The original of the present Convention, of which the Arabic, Chinese, English, French, Russian and Spanish texts are equally authentic, shall be deposited with the Secretary-General of the United Nations.

In witness thereof the undersigned plenipotentiaries, being duly authorized thereto by their respective Governments, have signed the present Convention.

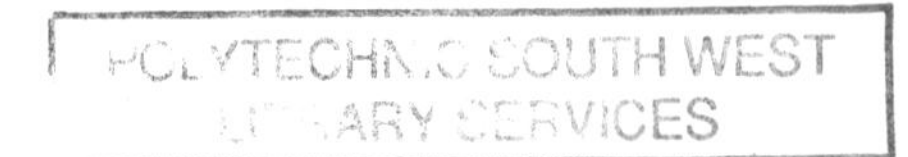